OUR
ATLANTIC
ATTEMPT

Commander Mackenzie Grieve, Mr T.O.M. Sopwith, C.B.E., Mrs Hawker and Mr H.G. Hawker

OUR ATLANTIC ATTEMPT

H.G. HAWKER &
K. MACKENZIE GRIEVE
With a new introduction by Malcolm Hall CEng MRAeS

NONSUCH

First published 1919
Copyright © in this edition Nonsuch Publishing, 2007
Introduction copyright © Malcolm Hall, 2007

Nonsuch Publishing
Cirencester Road, Chalford, Stroud, Gloucestershire, GL6 8PE
www.nonsuch-publishing.com

Nonsuch Publishing is an imprint of NPI Media Group

British Library Cataloguing in Publication Data.
A catalogue record for this book is available from the British Library.

ISBN 978 1 84588 603 5

Typesetting and origination by NPI Media Group
Printed in Great Britain

CONTENTS

INTRODUCTION TO
THE MODERN EDITION

Alfred Harmsworth, Viscount Northcliffe of the Isle of Thanet and owner of the *Daily Mail*, was one of the leaders in the birth of British popular journalism. In that guise, he was also one of the great benefactors of early British aviation. He began his crusade on its behalf in 1906, at a time when many still doubted that the Wrights had flown. That year he was visiting Paris and was present among the throng which had gathered to witness the Brazilian pioneer, Alberto Santos-Dumont, lurch into the air in his own version of a flying machine and fly in a straight line for a distance of some 220 metres. It was unimpressive compared with what we now know the Wrights had already achieved, but it impressed Northcliffe, who is said to have asserted that Britain was 'no longer an island'. Given that at that time no one else, either on that side of the English Channel or on this, had flown at all, Northcliffe could be accused of journalistic hyperbole. On the other hand, his words were to become endowed with prophetic significance when, three years later, Louis Blériot became the first man to fly across the Channel, in his Type XI monoplane, winning as he did so not only his place amongst the immortals, but also, at a more prosaic level, the £1,000 which Northcliffe, through the *Daily Mail*, had offered as a prize to the first man to accomplish the feat.

That prize was followed by others, as Northcliffe's way of encouraging the aeroplane's uncertain progress, including

£10,000 for the first pilot to fly from London to Manchester (won in 1910 by another Frenchman, Louis Paulhan, who beat the Englishman Claude Grahame-White in a contest of dramatic dimensions), gripped the nation's attention. As the aeroplane advanced, air shows (or 'meetings,' as they were called then) proliferated, as did aerial races, including the first *Daily Mail* Round-Britain Race, for a further £10,000, while the leading pilots were elevated by press and public to the level of national heroes.

In 1913 Northcliffe issued the greatest challenge of all when he offered yet another £10,000 to the first pilot who could fly across the broad Atlantic Ocean, non-stop, through its turbulent and cloud-encumbered skies. At the time, the world record for the longest distance flown by any aircraft stood at little more than 600 miles, although that was around a closed circuit, since long-distance flying from A to B still tended to be exceptional. As for the aircraft themselves, the design norm was represented by 100 mph biplanes propelled by single engines of low power and uncertain reliability, so it is small wonder that, by the time war broke out a year later, there had been no attempts to win the prize. For the next four years it lay in abeyance, while all the energies of the designers and pilots in the combatant nations were diverted to other purposes.

When peace returned, the scene had changed: in the fires of war, the aeroplane had been forged into a machine of a very different mettle from that of 1914. For the nation's aircraft manufacturers the target was now one which appeared attainable, while the renewal of Northcliffe's challenge came as a gleam of bright light in the gloomy tunnel down which they were then looking. For, with the signing of the Armistice, the flow of orders for fighting aircraft in large numbers, hitherto in flood, had been sharply turned off, and they had been in a very short time reduced to near-empty order books and idle workshops. Under these circumstances, competition was acute. For all concerned, it would be a race against time, with the team which was ready first standing the best chance of winning. There was no time to design a machine especially for the job: it would be necessary to take an existing design and adapt it to the task.

The contestants soon boiled down to four. Handley-Page and Vickers, having both produced large twin-engined aircraft with the range to bomb Germany from bases in France, looked perhaps the most promising. Sopwiths had tended to concentrate on shorter-range single-engined fighters such as the famous Camel, but had also designed a larger machine—the B.1 bomber—which they intended to modify for the attempt. The fourth contender, Martinsydes, had also been turning out aeroplanes for the war effort, including a not very successful fighter called the Buzzard, which formed the basis for their own entry.

As it happened, there was a fifth protagonist, in the shape of the United States Navy, which intended to attack the problem in its own way. For, although the Americans proposed to come to the party, they had decided to play by themselves. While all the other contenders naturally planned a course which would take them in the direction of the British Isles, the Americans chose to take a more southerly route, where they might hope for kinder weather than that to be encountered further north. Much more to the point, it would allow them to make an intermediate stop in the Azores before flying on another thousand miles to a European landfall at Lisbon. However, by adopting such a course, they would clearly make themselves ineligible for the *Daily Mail* prize—as well as forfeiting the greater kudos attached to the achievement of a non-stop crossing.

Their enterprise differed in other ways, too. Following a hallowed national tradition—at least in those days—all the British efforts were made by private companies—and not very wealthy ones at that. Not a penny of government money was involved. The American attempt, on the other hand, was an official Navy exercise and thus able to call on resources which were far beyond the reach of their British rivals. Rejoicing in such support, the project's planners based their schemes not on just a single aircraft, but on a whole flight—consisting of four Curtiss multi-engined flying boats. Furthermore, dozens of the Navy's warships were to be diverted from their normal duties and stationed at frequent intervals along the route, to act both as navigational markers and as rescue vessels in the event of any untoward incident. However, none of these arrangements need prevent them from claiming, quite justly and honourably, that they had conquered the mighty Atlantic.

Concerning two points, all taking part were in unanimous agreement. The crossing must be made from west to east, to take advantage of the prevailing tail winds which they might hope to expect. Furthermore, they all proposed to start from Newfoundland, which offered the attractive and added benefit of sticking out considerably further east than any suitable location on the Canadian mainland. By such means they could hope to minimise the number of anxious hours they would have to spend listening for any suspicious noises from the engine and watching the fuel gauge, often whilst uncertain of their position, with nothing but the trackless and unforthcoming ocean stretching beneath them in every direction.

The principal actor in the Sopwith attempt, Harry George Hawker, was already a household name, having been Tom Sopwith's chief pilot since before the war. He had landed in this country from his native Australia in May 1911, an impecunious twenty-two-year-old in need of a job. As a skilled mechanic, he found one in Sopwith's workshops at Brooklands, where the latter was just beginning to make his mark among the other pioneers whom history would in time recognise as the founders of the nation's aircraft manufacturing industry. Hawker himself soon raised his eyes higher than the workbench: he first persuaded Sopwith to teach him to fly, then in no time at all he had become the little company's main test pilot, as it advanced on the successful course which, when war came, culminated in the manufacture of thousands of aircraft for the Royal Flying Corps and the Royal Naval Air Service.

The story of the Sopwith team's dramatic failure to win Northcliffe's prize—which could so easily have been a success— is told in the following pages, with graceful understatement, by Hawker and his navigator, Lt-Cdr Kenneth Mackenzie Grieve, R.N. The chapters by the latter, concerning the navigational aspects of the flight, deserve as much attention from the reader as the description of the flight itself. While the diagrams and the technical explanations may not be to all readers' taste, their study is worth the effort, helping as it does to illuminate a picture of the discomforts which Grieve had to overcome, as well as his vital contribution to the near-success of their mission and indeed to the ultimate survival of himself and his pilot. Once out of sight of land and lacking all external navigational aids, including wireless, Grieve's task was continually to update his calculation of their position, based on airspeed, compass bearing, elapsed time and the speed and direction of the wayward wind. With accurate knowledge of the last-named critical to the maintenance of the desired course, yet with pre-flight forecasts unlikely to be accurate over such a long distance, regular verification of the current wind, by measurement of the 'drift,' as he describes it, represented another of his duties. Lastly, since, if he was lucky, he would have had the sun or the stars by which he could confirm or correct his calculations, he must from time to time employ the seaman's classic navigating instrument, the sextant, although, as Grieve explains, this part of his task was fraught with at least as much difficulty as the rest of it.

Picture then the stoical Grieve, huddled in his open cockpit, performing the calculations implied by his explanations of the problems involved, with gloved hands awkwardly marking courses and positions on his charts, and all the while with his mind distracted by the roar of the Rolls-Royce Eagle and his body chilled by the 100 mph sub-zero airflow snatching at his helmet and goggles. From time to time even the relative shelter of the cockpit must, as Hawker acknowledges, be abandoned, when Grieve was obliged to emerge into the full fury of the gale, in order to sight his sextant on a suitable star. Not for him today's air-conditioned flight deck and the benign assistance of inertial platform and satellite navigation!

Hawker's remarks supporting his preference for a single engine are also worthy of comment. Since he was obliged to use a single-engined machine for the attempt (from start to finish, the Sopwith company never produced anything else), it may well be that he was making a virtue of necessity. Yet, while it may have been specious, the view he expressed was not without logic at the time. At that point of aeronautical development, aircraft were still relatively under-powered and the ability of twin-engined machines to maintain level flight with one engine stopped would have been, to say the least, highly doubtful. Thus, argues Hawker, why accept the extra complication of two engines when, if one fails, the ultimate outcome is to be the same?

As for the engine breakdown which was the reason for the Sopwith's failure, the blame lay, of course, not with the Rolls-Royce engine itself, but with its associated cooling system. Although, in the relevant passage, Hawker expresses his belief that it was due to debris blocking the filter, in more recent years other theories for the overheating have been advanced to challenge this. One suggestion has been that of carburettor icing, insufficiently understood in those days, while another asserts that the linkage opening and closing the radiator blanking flap was connected up the wrong way around—a proposition which invokes the poignant picture of Hawker repeatedly making matters worse when, had he but known it, his salvation was under his hand.

By the time that Hawker and Grieve found themselves safe—though sorry—aboard the *Mary*, the Americans were in the Azores. Of the original flight of four flying boats, only three had been in a condition to set off from Newfoundland, while in the end only one of those, the NC4, had managed to complete the course. The other two had got lost on the way—despite the guiding chain of warships—and were wrecked when they landed in rough seas, fortunately without loss of life. Ten days later, on the evening of 27 May, at about the same time that Hawker and Grieve were being borne triumphantly through London from King's Cross station to the Royal Aero Club, and while Jack Alcock and Arthur Whitten-Brown were watching their converted Vickers Vimy bomber being assembled in Newfoundland, the NC4 and its crew finally landed at Lisbon harbour, allowing the American crew to claim the achievement of the first airborne crossing of the Atlantic Ocean.

Only nineteen more days were to pass before Alcock and Brown landed in Ireland in their Vimy, to complete the first non-stop crossing and earn for themselves the *Daily Mail* prize, knighthoods and eternal fame.

The other two contenders were non-starters, Fred Raynham literally so when he crashed in the Martinsyde, pluckily attempting to take off from an airfield which was even more inadequate than Hawker's an hour or two after the Sopwith's departure. The Handley-Page, on the other hand, was still unready when the Vimy took the prize, so it made the best of a bad job and went off in the opposite direction, to embark on a hastily-conceived sales tour of the US, which, after various mishaps, ended when it crashed at Cleveland.

The Atlantic adventure, with all its hazards, had ended successfully without the loss of a single life, but the gods were not to be denied the tribute which they were accustomed to claim as the price for such audacity. Barely six months after his triumph, Sir John Alcock was killed when he crashed in bad weather on a ferry flight in northern France. Only eighteen months after that tragedy Harry Hawker too lost his life, when the Nieuport Goshawk he was test-flying dived into the ground near Hendon aerodrome. They were neither the first nor the last of a not inconsiderable number of brave men who gave their lives to the conquest of the air. Their monument could be said to be, not just the steady stream of aircraft which today endlessly cross and re-cross the Atlantic, bearing their passengers to their destinations in safety and comfort, but the vast network of aerial communications across the world, which has shrunk its dimensions and of whose existence Hawker, Alcock and all their companions and contemporaries ninety years ago could never have dreamed.

Malcolm Hall C.Eng., M.R.Ae.S.
November 2007

PREFACE

BY MAJOR–GENERAL J.E.B. SEELY, D.S.O., C.M.G.
UNDER–SECRETARY FOR AIR

This little book of absorbing interest, written in modest and simple language, describes a very gallant exploit.

To set out on a voyage of 2000 miles over a stormy sea, in a craft which, however good for air travel, was not designed to live on the water, demanded courage of the highest order from Hawker and Grieve. In days to come, when the crossing of the Atlantic by air is an everyday occurrence, these dauntless pioneers who dared all for the honour of their country will not be forgotten.

John Edward Bernard Seely
Air Ministry
June 15, 1919

AUTHORS' NOTE

The authors of this little book desire to place on record their thanks to Captain Wilfrid Gordon Aston, R.A.F., A.F.R.AË S., A.M.I.A.E., for the help that he has afforded them in its compilation and in the reading of proofs.

H.G. Hawker
K. Mackenzie Grieve

I

THE VIMY SUCCESS

Since this little book was got together we have received news of the magnificent success which has been achieved by the Vickers 'Vimy' Rolls-Royce biplane, piloted by Capt. Sir J. Alcock and navigated by Lieut. Sir A. Witten Brown. What little we have seen of the Atlantic only inspires us with greater appreciation for this splendid performance, which will justly take its place as one of the outstanding milestones of British Aviation. It is a triumph of pilotage, triumph of navigation, and a triumph for the British aeroplane and the British aircraft engine, beside which all previous aeronautical performances shrink almost into insignificance.

We respectfully offer our heartiest congratulations.

H.G. Hawker
K. Mackenzie Grieve

II

GENERAL INTRODUCTION

BY CAPTAIN W. GORDON ASTON, R.A.F.,
A.F.R.AË.S., A.M.I.A.E.

It would be difficult indeed to imagine a more dramatic turn of events than that which converted, on 20th May 1919, that which was purely and simply a strenuous struggle for a great money prize into an International Competition in which men were ready to risk their lives, to give them cheerfully, if necessary, in order that the pride of their own country might be honourably upheld.

One looks around in vain for a parallel to the reception with which Mr Hawker and Lieut.-Commander Mackenzie Grieve were welcomed upon their return from what most of the public had quickly come to regard as 'the dead.' Yet at the same time one looks around, also in vain, for a parallel to their performance. By no means wanting is the crew of melancholy croakers who would have it that this extraordinary acclamation was out of all proportion, was—if one can forget that some of those who are so desperately critical may have the taste sour grapes in their mouths—a monstrous illustration of the ill-guided power of the Press, was an insult to the honour and fair name of fighting men who have, after months and years of magnificent warfare, returned home to find themselves confronted by a crowd less enthusiastic and smaller in numbers than that which carried Hawker and Grieve shoulder-high at

King's Cross on Tuesday, 27th May. And from this they would draw a comparison.

Now comparisons are all very well. By reputation they are odious, and in this case they are utterly futile. The individual gallantry and the personal heroism which have been lavished in France, in Gallipoli, in Mesopotamia, in the almost innumerable theatres of a world-war are beyond the capacity of tongue or pen to describe, and not a whit less to be revered and renowned because for the most part their deeds have been done in hot blood. Does anybody seriously suggest that the country has failed to appreciate what has been one for its sake?

But there is a great gulf of difference between Westminster Abbey and King's Cross, and that which will merit a niche in the one will not necessarily, by any means, draw a crowd to the other.

It is desirable that a proper sense of proportion should be retained. Those who seek an explanation or an unprecedented display of public enthusiasm in the influence which is wielded by one particular section of the Daily Press give it credit for a power which it most certainly does not possess, and which it would find exceedingly inconvenient to manage if it had it. The great British public was never encouraged by any newspaper campaign to swarm on to the platforms of stations at which the Scotch Express did not stop, any more than the same agency was responsible for making signalmen repudiate railway regulations and lay fog bombs on rails that had nothing but pellucid blue between their polished surface and heaven. Pilots do not take up 'D.H.9's' for escort purposes because their morning newspapers tell them to do so. But all these things are done when they spring from natural enthusiasm. That they are done for returning aviators who have got little more than a ducking in the Atlantic to show for their trouble, and that they are not done for a Pullman car load of a triumphantly returning General Staff admits of a very ready and very simple explanation, and I have no hesitation in dealing with it because, if it has occurred to anyone else, it does not seem to have been enlarged upon as it should have been.

When Field-Marshal Sir Douglas Haig arrived but recently at Victoria Station he was met by a decorous crowd of several thousand people, who raised their hats to him, reverently thanked Gods for Scotland, and whether they were Socialists, Bolshevists, members of the Independent Labour Party, or just ordinary honest London citizens, felt that here was a man fit for an Earldom at the very least, who would confer a greater dignity upon the House of Lords than even the Peerage was likely to confer upon him.

Has anyone ever suggested that Mr Hawker or Commander Mackenzie Grieve ought to be forthwith given a barony? Has anyone ever put forward the notion that Lord Hawker of Hook and Lord Grieve of Droxford, in the county of Hampshire, should forthwith be translated to the Upper Chamber?

What then is the psychology of this affair? What reason can be found for the fact that one kind of work demands a recognition that in the form of a hereditary title shall last into to the thirtieth or fortieth generation, and yet will not draw a crowd; and that another kind, no less *pro patria* in essence, shall tie no labels to any man's neck, and yet stop the traffic from Islington to Mayfair? Something Big has got to be done for motor omnibuses to be running down Vigo Street. And yet it is a Something Big that leaves the man a plain Mister.

The answer to this conundrum is exceedingly simple in the light of the argument that has been suggested. The British public, in common with all other publics in the world, has an intense awe, admiration, and reverence for the great things which it never pretends to understand. In spite of the tips it has received from innumerable amateur tacticians it knows a little less than nothing about the administration of Military and Naval warfare. It realises that Field-Marshal Sir Douglas Haig and Admiral Sir David Beatty are super-men, because it is dimly conscious of the fact that Great Britain has not been successfully invaded—in the warlike sense—by the Hun. It therefore takes off its hat, literally and metaphorically, to these heroes, and later on it will manifest its awe, admiration, and reverence of them by enshrining their lithographic likenesses in its parlours. But like Mr Gladstone and Lord Beaconsfield, these men are national gods who will be worshipped in a remote sort of way. The work they have done, the difficulties they had to contend with, the profundities of administering a nation in arms are not easily understanded of the people. Those who have been to the Staff College, those who have wandered in the mazes of Whitehall, have a glimmering of all these things and realise the magnitude of Haig's and Beatty's tasks. It is they who, in their thousands, made a pilgrimage to meet the Folkestone train at Victoria.

I shall not now say that they who gravitated in their hundreds of thousands to King's Cross did so because they understood the difficulties of the transatlantic flight, and were anxious to do homage to men who had done their best to set these difficulties at nought. Far from it. Truth to tell the great British public is rather more ignorant of aeronautics on a grand scale than it is of military strategy—and that is saying a good deal. But it occasionally sees a map and it realises very thoroughly that the Atlantic Ocean is a very large place indeed, that England is really a very small Island, and that the United States of America is very, very, long way off. From the one fact it derives a large measure of its justifiable national pride; by the other it is led to believe that there is more in the Monroe Doctrine than meets the eye.

The great British public is very well informed, too, of the dangers of flying. Singularly enough, the very newspapers which have done so much to encourage progress in aviation and thereby earned he gratitude of every thinking man and woman in the Empire have been the very media through which it has learnt of the toll of life and limb that this progress has exacted, and still, alas! exacts. But that, after all, is perhaps just as well. It is highly desirable that these things should be known, for aviation is a plant that has to be developed into a hardy annual, it could never hope to flourish as an exotic in the hush-hush atmosphere of a hothouse.

Primarily, then, people knew that a flight across the Atlantic was a big thing. It came to their minds that liners took a week, even in peace-time before the War, to go from New York to Liverpool at five-and-twenty knots. It grew upon them that when a couple of men in an aeroplane set themselves to do battle with two thousand miles of unknown elements they have taken a job in hand which is, to say the least, an extraordinarily sporting proposition. And finally they realised that from the moment that the machine left the hospitable ground and launched itself into the supra-Atlantic air it had severed its connexion with succour of almost ally kind, cut its communications with the rest of humanity, and burnt its boats with a vengeance.

I am one of those who believe that if Hawker and Grieve had come through without a hitch according to programme, and landed at Brooklands as it was their ultimate intention of doing, they would have been the recipients of an ovation quite trifling in comparison with what they actually received as a result of their glorious failure. For the immensity of their task was never within miles of being realised until the lack of definite news pointed to the probability of their being lost. It was only then that the man in the club and the man in the workshop began to see the infinite possibilities of what might have happened; it was only then that people began to blame the Admiralty for not smothering the ocean with ships.

The fact of the matter is that nothing succeeds like success. We hear, without a thrill and with the merest approach to surprise,

The crowd at King's Cross. Puzzle, find Hawker and Grieve!

that nowadays a wireless telephone permits us to conduct a commonplace conversation with somebody in an airship fifty miles away. Only the least *blasé* of us says so much as 'How wonderful!' We are, for the most part, utterly unsympathetic to the whole thing, knowing nothing and caring less about the problems which have had to be solved, and of the dead failures whose bones have only served to pave the path of success. It is probable that at least two score of courageous scientists have been working night and day upon wireless telephony for the last twenty years, but it is only in the obscure archives of a learned society that you will read of their pyramidal, rather than monumental efforts. Their failures were the failures of the laboratory. Interesting to the savant, but otherwise hopeless as a news item. Now Hawker and Grieve's failure was a spectacular affair. If they had succeeded, people would have said 'How wonderful! They have flown the Atlantic! what's-his-name will get ten thousand pounds. I must get a paper and see how old Clemenceau is soaking Brockdorff-Rantzau.'

But because they did *not* succeed, it was 'Good God! they *haven't* flown the Atlantic! What's become of them? These infernal papers tell one nothing!'

And then, almost unconsciously, they began to see what a flight across the Atlantic in a 'land' aeroplane really meant. Or at all events they began to figure what their own feelings would be if they found themselves suspended in the sky with a couple of thousand miles of cold, relentless sea to cover ere ever they got back to their native element again.

It is notable that the arrival of Hawker and Grieve in London coincided with a remarkable rally of Service men. This rally was a quite informal affair, and took place simply because Hawker and Grieve *were* arriving. I am aware that the Aussies, as contemporary history shows, took a commanding part in the reception; that is because of a way the Aussies have, but no particularly minute observation was needed to make clear the fact that khaki and silver-badge predominated in the crowd. The reason for that is obvious enough. These were men to whom the circumstances of single-handed combat had grown familiar. They went to welcome Hawker and Grieve because they recognised those circumstances in the fight with the Atlantic distance and the Atlantic darkness. They were swift to perceive in the aviators kindred spirits, brother-embracers of the sporting chance!

It has been said that Hawker and Grieve became popular heroes simply because they rose, as it were, from the dead, and that it was only natural ttat people should flock to 'chair' the living oldies of men who they had satisfied themselves must for several days have been corpses. I am disinclined to take that view. The blank silence and fruitless speculation of a week served to focus attention upon what appeared to be a vivid tragedy, but cannot see that it did more than that, except in so far as it encouraged one's mind to visualise the grim helplessness of an insignificant aeroplane lost in a waste of waters. The better informed were well aware that 'no news is often good news.' Had the worst happened some fragmentary trace would have surely remained of the disaster! The ocean is big, but the wonderful conduct of a submarine campaign had shown that a seaman's eyes are incredibly keen, and if further evidence be required of this the fact that the Sopwith machine was eventually salved supplies it.

No! The thing that appealed to every heart was this (and there will never be much the matter with Britain so long as the same thing makes the same appeal): it was a straightforward 'heads I win, tails I lose' proposition, with, if anything, a strong bias towards the coin turning up 'tails.' £10,000 is a good round sum of money. It conveys the comfortable assurance of £500 a year (less income tax), and is a lump sum competence to which most of us aspire in vain, but nevertheless aspire. Two thousand miles of flying would win it, and how many millions of mathematicians came to the conclusion that £5 a mile wasn't bad going. But one casts one's mind back to the early clays of aviation, when Moore-Brabazon got £1000 a mile for a mile flight, when Blériot got £400 a mile for his Cross-Channel trip, when Paulhan got £25 a mile for London to Manchester, and one began to think that something under three-farthings a yard wasn't so very much after all. Still, it was a fine new form of competition, an excellent topic by way of an antidote to the Peace Conference, and wholly and hugely interesting. It was, in fact, more interesting to the public than a prize fight for a purse of similar value, for tucked away at the back of the public's heart is a sort of conviction that the War was won in the Air, and that aeronautical progress meant more than something to an Island Nation that was little likely to remain inviolable by air unless progress were continued.

In the earlier period of the *Daily Mail* Competition it appeared to be a 'snip' for Britain. Mr Hugo Sunstedt of U.S.A. was early in the field and caused a mild, though unfortunately smothered, flutter of excitement, after which it was purely the playing of a waiting game. In England an almost unprecedented succession of cloudless days made it difficult to believe that out in mid-Atlantic, and on or about a straight line ruled on the map between St. John's and Brooklands, 'south-westerly depressions' and similar absurdities were preventing Mr Hawker and his navigator from taking the air. When the Sopwith crew positively allowed Mr Raynham and Captain Morgan to put their Martinsyde machine together, the Man in the Underground began to worry about it. He poked his head out of his office window, concluded there was 'nothing wrong with the weather, anyhow' and wondered how on earth people could not bother to pick up a fortune when there it was, at Carmelite House, for the asking. Of course, he read the weather reports, but as he did not understand them in terms of words and figures and was perfectly lost when he saw them graphically represented in charts, he was not particularly impressed. The idea of a race between the 'Atlantic' and the 'Raymor' did get home on him, however, and there are records of tentative odds having been snapped up.

The fact is, the British public were getting rather tired of waiting; but, as it very well knew in its heart, it was not half so tired of waiting as the aviators at St. John's. By virtue of its interest it has increased its knowledge enormously. Formerly it associated Newfoundland with cod-liver oil and wood-pulp for paper manufacture. Now it knows that the staple product of that state is fog. And suddenly, behind the fog, loomed the huge bulk of the American Navy with its deliberate flying boats.

'The NC 1, NC 2, NC 3, and NC 4 have arrived at Trepassey,' read the man in the Tube. 'Hawker and Raynham will be starting this afternoon.'

Hawker and Raynham didn't start.

The trivial fact that their direct route lay East and by North had a good deal to do with it.

'The NC 1, the NC 3 and the NC 4 have started for the Azores. Hawker and Raynham will have to look sharp!'

Hawker and Raynham did trial flights only.

The fact that the seaplanes' route lay East and by South had something to do with it.

'The NC 4 has arrived at the Azores! Can Hawker and Raynham catch it up?'

Hawker and Raynham started.

But the £10,000 Prize had got nothing to do with it!

The human being is extraordinarily susceptible to the dramatic, particularly if it happens to be a British human being. Plays which, in the ' book,' are palpably worthless run a thousand-and-one nights because they contain, in some hidden corner, that peculiar dramatic twist which uproots the least firmly established emotions. It is safe to say that no human being, with eyes capable of reading newspaper, failed to react to the dramatic touch Hawker's start.

For weeks they had been waiting in Newfoundland for a favourable turn in the weather which showed no great hurry to make its appearance, but this was natural enough, as until midsummer the weather in that latitude is rarely good. So far as the competition for the £10,000 prize was concerned they were quite prepared to wait for a very considerable period. No American competitor was to be feared now that Mr Sunstedt was *hors de combat*, nor did they need to look for a surprise from another British competitor, for the Short machine which was to start from Ireland had come to grief in its journey from Eastchurch to Limerick, and it was extremely unlikely that it could be made ready for another attempt for some weeks. In any case they would hear of its preparation for a second flight, and the fact that it would be travelling from East to West, and consequently against the prevailing Atlantic wind, would slow it down so much that even if both machines started at the same moment they could, all being well, reach Ireland several hours before the Short machine could get to America. Mr Raynham and Captain Morgan, with their Martinsyde 'Raymor,' had arrived in Newfoundland not very long after Mr Hawker and Lieut.-Commander Grieve, but the pilots of the two rival aeroplanes had quickly reached an amicable agreement that neither should steal a march on the other, but that either side should give warning of its intention to start. The four-engined Handley-Page was being erected in Newfoundland and the packing-cases of the Vickers 'Vimy' were expected at any moment, but since their machines were complete and well tested neither Mr Hawker nor Mr Raynham had any need to worry, and theirs being the fastest machines they could both equally afford to wait, for whatever weather suited the other entrants would just as well suit them. On the other hand, they were very well acquainted with the stupendous difficulties that lay in front of them, and so long as the prize alone were at issue they were not going to start until the most favourable weather came along from which they could get the greatest possible help.

But the whole complexion of affairs was changed when the American flying boats started from Trepassey. They were not taking part in the £10,000 competition, but they were very definitely out to be the first aeroplanes to fly across the Atlantic. Their announced course was to Plymouth, via Lisbon and the Azores, and the weather reports all went to show that on the longest 'leg' of the course, that is to say from Trepassey to the Azores, they would, in all probability, be steadily running into increasingly good weather. The seaplanes could, therefore, in the event of any mishap, come down on to the surface of the ocean, and any risk of their being lost was almost entirely avoided by the fact that they were in constant touch, by wireless, with a large number of vessels which the U.S. Navy had sent out to mark the course and act as guides.

The American effort lacked nothing that careful and lavish organisation could give it, and it became at once clear to the crews of the Sopwith and Martinsyde machines that the seaplanes were formidable rivals, not for the money prize, but for the honour of being first across.

The only consolation was that they were slow and the British machines were fast, but by the time the NC 4 had reached the Azores this discrepancy, favourable to Hawker and Raynham, had ceased to exist.

Within a few hours the conditions had utterly changed. It was no longer a question of taking their time about it. It was a question of now or never.

Mr Hawker, Lieut.-Commander Grieve, Mr Raynham, and Captain Morgan unhesitatingly voted for a decisive 'now!' and as soon as a suitable hour had arrived—for it was necessary to start at such a time as would ensure daylight long before Ireland could be reached—Hawker and Grieve, with the full load of petrol, oil, mails, cinema films, and food aboard their aeroplane were in the air on their great journey, whilst Raynham and Morgan were making energetic preparations to follow them at once. They could afford a little time, however, as the Martinsyde was slightly faster than the Sopwith.

In getting off as they did these very gallant gentlemen performed an act of such intense daring and single-minded patriotism that an instant chord was struck in the responsive heart of every Briton, and indeed of every unit of every race the world over. The difficulties of the Atlantic flight might be under-rated or over-rated, according to the direction in which lack of full knowledge might bend the opinion, but the heroism of this dramatic action was transparently obvious.

To start with, the weather reports were definitely unfavourable, more so than they had been on many previous occasions. They had counted on favourable weather, and originally were not prepared to push off without it. Yet they had taken their chance without any hesitation whatever.

The American machines which they were out to beat at all costs had the avowed intention of crossing the ocean by means of a series of 'hops,' whereas the Sopwith and the Martinsyde, being 'land' aeroplanes, had set themselves the task of travelling from the New World to the Old in one mighty non-stop flight. Supposing Hawker and Grieve had let the seaplanes go unchallenged, had let them get to Plymouth, it would do them personally no harm whatever, and so far as national pride was concerned the immensely greater feat of a subsequent non-stop flight would be apparent to the meanest intelligence. Less courageous or less patriotic men might have, and justifiably, been content to say, 'It is not good enough. Let them get there by "hops." Let America have the honour of being the first to fly the Atlantic. They have adopted the easier way. We will wait for the right kind of wind and ensure that Great Britain has the honour of having the first aeroplane to fly, non-stop, from one side of the ocean to the other.' It is quite safe to say that if the British competitors had not started, not a single tongue or pen in Great Britain would have criticised their inaction. On the contrary, it is more than probable that an even greater measure of sympathy would have been accorded them in that the chance had been snatched from them in a manner to which a reply was prevented by sheer force of circumstances.

But whatever interested persons may have thought in Great Britain, it is manifest that no such notions were ever entertained by any of the British aviators in Newfoundland. Only one thing mattered, and that was the national pride of being first across, prize or no prize, hop or non-stop.

All the difficulties were brushed on one side or completely forgotten. The exiguous aerodrome (Newfoundland is by nature one of the worst countries for flying conceivable) which demanded that for a safe 'get off' the wind should be in a certain definite direction—which it was not. The bad weather that the crew knew they had to face, for only an astonishing stroke of luck could enable them to avoid it. A 'chancy' wireless set, the need for which would be so much the greater if the weather were against the taking of accurate astronomical observations. Singly these troubles were not so bad, but together they furnished a formidable combination—a combination, moreover, to be viewed in cold blood.

Hawker and Grieve 'took' that combination 'on' without a moment's hesitation, and with none of the assurance of ignorance, for they were perfectly well aware of the odds against them. Their minds were made up, and it was going to be through no fault of their own if the gigantic—the almost hopeless—task were not accomplished.

Small wonder that they are firmly enshrined as heroes in every heart, and more particularly firmly in those hearts that, loving sport for sports' sake, realise that the essence of sport is the acceptance of adverse odds, and the playing of the up-hill game. Heirs of the spirit of Grenville, Franklin Scott, Evans, and of all the noble band of gentlemen adventurers, upholders of the great traditions that have made the British Empire what it is, H.G. Hawker and Lieut.-Commander K. Mackenzie Grieve have gained a permanent place in history from which nothing can ever dislodge them.

They themselves tell you in this book how they failed in a great feat of aviation, but those who read between the lines will see that in the Greater Game they attained a magnificent success. Few failures have been so great a triumph.

For, beaten in Time
From the start to the finish,
So utterly beaten
Appeal is impossible,
The spirit of man,
Enquiring, aspiring,
Passionately scaling
Ice-bitten altitudes,
Neighboured of none
Save the austere,
Unapproachable stars;
Scapes from its destiny,
Holds on its course
Of attest and discovery,
So as to leave,
When the Lord takes it back to Him,
The lot of the world
Something the prouder,
Something the loftier,
Something the braver,
For that it hath done.

From *A Song of Speed*, dedicated to Alfred Harmsworth by
W.E. Henley

III

THE DAILY MAIL *COMPETITIONS*

BY H.G. HAWKER

If there is one thing more than another which I desire to make clear in this little book, it is my intense admiration for the enterprise; and public spirit of the *Daily Mail*, and my enduring gratitude for the handsome and generous manner in which they have treated me. I have taken part in two of the great competitions which they have promoted and failed in both, and yet been made the recipient in each case of a magnificent consolation prize. In the Round Britain flight, in which with Kauper as passenger I flew a Sopwith machine in August 1913, we came to grief off the coast of Ireland, and so failed to win the prize of £5000 which the *Daily Mail* had offered for this flight, but they immediately came forward and presented me with a cheque for £1000 as a consolation prize. In the case of this Atlantic failure; not only do they present Grieve and myself with £5000, a munificent consolation prize, but, as I think shows their generosity even to a greater extent, whilst we were lost upon the Atlantic and when our fate was in considerable doubt and the odds against our safe return must have seemed to be very strong, they announced their intention of giving the full value of the prize, namely £10,000, to the families of Grieve and myself.

It is not my purpose to use this little book as a medium for expressing my personal gratitude to the proprietors of the *Daily*

Mail, but I cannot possibly let this opportunity pass without confirming my considered conviction that these enterprising gentlemen have done more for British aviation than any other people in the world, and that it is largely to the progress that has been made under the stimulus of the competitions they have promoted that the present commanding position of Great Britain in the world of aeronautics is directly due. As a case in point, the *Daily Mail* put up a prize of £1000 for the first British aeroplane manned by a British pilot which flew a British mile. This prize was won by Colonel T.C. Moore-Brabazon, R.A.F., now MP for Chatham, and lately head of the photographic section at the Air Ministry. On 25th July 1909, they announced a prize of £1000 for the first flight across the Channel, which was won by Mons. Louis Blériot, on his monoplane. No sooner had this sum of money been collected from them than they put forward another great prize of £1,000 for a flight from London to Manchester; after a gallant attempt by Grahame White, this was won by Louis Paulhan on 28th April 1910. They next promoted the Circuit of Britain flight and the Round Britain 'Seaplane' flight, and as a culmination offered a great prize of £10,000 for a flight across the Atlantic. I have no doubt that by the time these lines see daylight this prize will have been won, and I suppose that it is more than likely that yet another munificent sum of money will have been offered as an inducement to the development of British aeronautical enterprise.

The fact of these large sums of money having been given to an industry which before the war was largely in a state of starvation is perfectly wonderful, for it showed as nothing else did that aviation during its long process of, I almost might say thankless and unrequited development, was not without influential support in high places. Whether the Government ought to have done what Lord Northcliffe did is a matter of secondary importance beside the fact that, at all events, someone came forward with a material and valuable form of patronage.

Personally, I have always been extremely keen on competitions, and have thoroughly realised their value, not only in stimulating enterprise, but also in advertising flying. That aviation will become a matter of the closest concern of the ordinary public of the future admits of no doubt whatever. It is a form of transport the conditions of which are so advantageous that it is only a question of time before it comes into common use for all sorts of purposes, many of which we do not perhaps realise at the present time. But the rate at which it develops and the extent to which it develops are alike dependent upon public support, and to get this the whole aviation movement has got to be gushed forward by every conceivable means. The man in the street must be made to realise the importance of flying, not only to the wealthy joyrider, but also to himself, for every means of transport that has for its object the minimising of delay and the shortening of distance is of immediate importance to every one of us. I don't suppose that I can claim that our unfortunate Atlantic attempt was in itself a good advertisement or flying, yet if the circumstances of that attempt are analysed, I think that an earnest is given for what aviation can do in the future. The mishap that brought us down was a trifling one, although had just the same effect as though we had broken a crankshaft or some other vital part had failed. But is it not certain that within a very short while water circulation systems will be such that they can never go wrong? At all events, nothing was done to indicate that neither aeroplanes nor aircraft engines can be relied upon to go on working almost indefinitely.

IV

PREPARATIONS IN NEWFOUNDLAND

BY H.G. HAWKER

Grieve and I, accompanied by Green the Rolls-Royce expert, and Engholm the cinema man from Messrs Jury's, Ltd., left England in the *Digby* on 10th March, with our machine carefully packed into two big crates and a few small cases. We arrived in Placentia Bay on the 28th, and trans-shipped to the *Portia*, which landed our impedimenta and ourselves at Placentia, from where we went on by train to St. John's. The trans-shipping of the machine was rendered necessary by the fact that St. John's was packed up with Arctic ice. Captain Montague Fenn and his ground staff had gone over previously, and had already chosen an aerodrome and had an excellent wooden shed erected before we arrived. This was built of rough lumber, but was much to be preferred to the tent which had been taken over in case of need, as the weather was very bad, and as a matter of fact the whole place was under snow.

This made the choosing of an aerodrome a matter of great difficulty, but Captain Fenn certainly got the very best place available. I am sure, however, the many excellent friends we made in Newfoundland will not accuse me of slighting their hospitable country when I say that it is the last place in which one would look for spacious landing grounds. Of course we knew this pretty well from maps before we started, but if anything the maps seemed to flatter the country, and actually, from the aerodrome point of view, it was a little worse than I had expected. All along I had well realised that the aerodrome difficulty would probably be the worst we should have to contend with, for, to start with, the nature of the country made it probable that we could not get much smooth ground in one patch, and, in the second place, it was necessary that before we started off in earnest we should want to make several trial flights for one purpose or another, and to do these we should be very much dependent upon the wind direction. We certainly could not afford to risk damaging the aeroplane by attempting trial flights under bad conditions. As a matter of fact, it was this very consideration that made it impossible for us thoroughly to test in the air the second wireless set which was sent out to us, for between its arrival and our start there was not a day on which we could have made a flight with any degree of certainty about a landing.

The aerodrome was an L-shaped piece of ground about 400 yards on its longest limb, and about 200 yards along the shorter. The long part of the L faced roughly east and west, and the short part north and south, the latter being at the eastern end. The L shape was due to the fact that the ground skirted a hill about 200 feet high with pretty steep sides. The ground had long been under snow, and as might have been supposed was almost entirely innocent of drainage. The short limb was strongly uphill from the south, at which end it had high trees, and there were low trees at each end of the long limb. It was fairly all right for starting in a due east wind, though in these circumstances we had to start off from soft and boggy ground, than which it is possible to imagine nothing more dangerous. With a west wind we should finish our run in the soft ground, and would also be running uphill. Had our machine been lightly loaded it would not have been

General view of St John's, Newfoundland

necessary to think about things to such an extent, but as it was we had to be very careful indeed.

The aerodrome was about 450 feet above sea level and seemed to catch all the sorts of winds that we did not want. It was about six miles from St. John's, which was its nearest point on the coast. This made it a little awkward to get labour for the improvements which Captain Fenn had got in hand, but at one time we had a gang of about sixty men busily filling up the worst of the soft places. Needless to say, any sort of a get off was impossible when the ground was covered with snow.

The trial flights of our aeroplane at Brooklands had been done mostly with a four-bladed propeller, but it was decided in Newfoundland to use the two-blader which we had taken over, as this gave a little more thrust, and though we had to pay for that with a trifling reduction in speed it was better to make sure of getting out of the ground.

Our original intention when we left England was, if possible, to get away before anyone else came on the scene, but this scheme was quickly seen to be out of the question on account not only of unfavourable winds, but also on account of the softness of the aerodrome and heavy snowfalls. So it soon became clear that we should have to possess our souls in patience and simply wait.

For sheer agony waiting on a job like ours was about the limit. Newfoundland is not a fashionable watering-place with a thousand and one things going on, though of course Grieve and I remember with intense gratitude the great kindness and hospitality which were shown us on all sides. But even if it had been the most entertaining place in the world, we should have

Testing the life saving suits

still found it irksome, because we just wanted to get the thing over and done with as soon as possible. I'm a little afraid that sometimes the enforced idleness got on our tempers.

But as a matter of fact we had always got something to do. Every day we used to go up to the aerodrome in a car which sometimes provided amusement by getting firmly stuck in deep snowdrifts from which it had to be dug out. Then there was always some titivation to be done on the machine, the engine run to see that all was well, the wireless set experimented with, and the water emptied in and out of the circulation system to prevent any chance of the motor freezing. The machine had taken about a week to erect, and at any time after that we were always ready to push off at, at most, a couple of hours' notice— just time enough to get the tanks filled up, the mail aboard, the thermos flasks filled, and the engine nicely warmed up.

It is quite probable that putting water in and out of the engine helped towards our eventual failure by causing more rust to form in the circulation system than would otherwise be the case. If so, then it just shows that you can be too careful in matters of this kind.

We had a certain amount of fun in unshipping our boat and testing it on a lake, when it behaved very well indeed, and in the same water we gave our suits a trial run. These were thoroughly waterproof, coming tight round the wrists and round the neck, where they were attached to a strong yoke, and being lined with kapok. They were very nice and warm and under test they showed their ability to keep the water out pretty well. They had originally been filled with kapok, but we took this material out and added air bags instead, which were lighter, and could be immediately blown up by mouth.

Raynham and Morgan arrived with their Martinsyde on 10th April, and lost no time in getting it together. They had had representatives over before ours lead been in Newfoundland to choose an aerodrome, but in our opinion their ground was

Testing the detachable boat

not so good as ours, as it was very narrow and only suitable for getting off in a south-westerly or westerly wind.

We were all of us staying at the same hotel—the Cochrane House—in St. John's, and we were and always had been the best of friends, but there was no one else in the field so far as we could see, and we settled down into watching one another like a cat watches a mouse. We indulged in plenty of practical jokes to liven up the time, we visited the meteorological station together, we ate ices at the local druggist's—Mr Pedigrew—and we both sympathised (though personally I have been a teetotaller and non-smoker all my life) with the unfortunates who still found total prohibition not quite to their taste.

But it soon began to seem hardly good enough. After all, we were there on the same errand, we had both got to do our best for British aviation, and was going to be no good being on tenterhooks the whole time—waiting was bad enough for all of us anyhow. So one day we quickly arrived at a very simple mutual agreement. We would each give the other a couple of hours' notice before starting, and the same time to the wireless people so as to enable them to get their warnings out broadcast to ships, and by that means the atmosphere was rendered a little less electrical. In any case, there wasn't very much difference in the speed of the machines, and if we both got away together, well, at all events, we could keep each other company part of the way at any rate, and we never knew but what we might be of mutual help.

In the meantime the weather was uniformly rotten. Sometimes it would clear up a bit and look promising, but the reports from the meteorological station almost always continued to put a different complexion on it. The thick white fogs would, whenever the wind went into the east, roll in from the banks and smother us. One felt sometimes like having a go in spite of them, but our aerodrome was not the sort of ground one could negotiate blindfold.

Then on the Friday evening we heard that the three NC machines had arrived at Trepassey. This was a good long way off, and the road bad, otherwise we should have liked to have gone over to see them. Their coming sharpened the tension up again and made the waiting game still less attractive than ever; for they were going to steer a southerly course and we a northerly one; they were going to improve the weather with every mile they went, and the odds were that we should find it getting worse. In any case, they brought in the international element, although they were not eligible for the *Daily Mail* prize, and what was very evident from the first was that they meant serious business. We speedily saw that they meant getting across first at all costs, also that they meant going soon.

But so far as speed was concerned we had got a fair margin in hand, and we reckoned that if we started from Newfoundland as soon as possible after they reached the Azores we should still have plenty of chance, and anyhow there couldn't be any stopping midway as far as we were concerned.

Several people have wondered why we didn't simply push off to the Azores after them, as if we had kept an under-carriage on the machine we could have landed there. For one thing we had not got a store of petrol on those islands for the replenishment of our tanks, and for another we should probably have had more than a little difficulty in finding the Azores at all. But primarily and finally, we had arranged to do the trip in one flight only; given reasonable weather we knew we could do it (or thought we could at any rate) and anyhow that was the way we were going to do it.

On the Friday evening, 16th May, the NC's got away, and all day long we waited for news with, I need hardly say, great anxiety, for Raynham and Morgan and Grieve and I had already made up our minds. On the Saturday evening we got the unconfirmed report that all three seaplanes, the NC 2, the NC 3, and the NC 4 had safely arrived at the Azores.

After that there was only one thing to do, namely, get as much sleep as we could, for we didn't intend to have any the following night. We meant having something more interesting on hand.

V

THE FAILURE

BY H.G. HAWKER

Early on Sunday, 18th May, the Sopwith 'Atlantic' aeroplane was all ready, tanks filled, and everything aboard, and after saying 'au revoir' to all our friends, sending our respects (and hopes of seeing him at Brooklands) to Raynham, and getting the Rolls-Royce engine nicely warmed up and ticking over contentedly, we got in and pushed off at 5.42 p.m. Greenwich time, that is 3.40 p.m. Newfoundland local summer time. Getting off was just a bit ticklish. The wind was about twenty miles an hour east-north-east, and that meant that we had got to go diagonally across our L-shaped ground, just touching the hill that I have mentioned, and avoiding, if we could, a deepish drainage ditch which ran along the foot of it. All our trial flights both in England and in Newfoundland had been done with three-quarter load of petrol, and we knew very well that there would not be too much room with the full load on board. However, all was well. The going was rough and the hillside made her roll a bit, but we missed the ditch by inches and got into the air all right with a respectable distance to spare between our wheels and the trees. As soon as we were well up I throttled down and we started a steady climb out towards the Atlantic and towards the Ireland that we hoped to see inside the next twenty four hours.

As soon as the coast had been passed, I pulled the under-carriage release trigger and away it went into the water.

Simultaneously the finger of the air speed indicator went over to another seven miles an hour.

The sky was bright and clear to start with, but we had not got up many thousand feet, and I think had only been flying about ten minutes when we saw that Newfoundland's staple product—fog—was hanging on to her coasts. But that didn't worry us very much. The fog is never more than a few hundred feet thick, and we knew we should soon be leaving it behind. Grieve had been able to observe the sea long enough to get a fair drift reading, and the fog bank didn't interfere with his navigation as it gave him the sort of horizon he wanted, being quite flat and distinct.

As far as the weather was concerned everything looked quite nice for some hours. We were comfortably jogging along at about 10,000 feet with nothing much in the way of cloud between ourselves and the vault of heaven, with the engine roaring contentedly as though it did not mean to misfire until the tanks were bone dry, and with the air speed indicator showing a decent 105 miles an hour. There were practically no bumps, and I could pretty well let the machine fly itself so long I held her on the course that Grieve had laid down.

About 10 o'clock all the blue in the sky had turned to purple, the warm glint of the sun had faded from the polished edges of the struts, and the clouds below us became dull and patchy and grey, only giving us very infrequently a sight of the ocean beneath them.

A quarter of an hour later the weather conditions had noticeably changed for the worse. The sky became hazy and thick so that we could not see anything below us with any distinctness, but we could perceive clearly enough that there was some pretty heavy stuff ahead. However, there was only one thing to do. It wasn't very solid so we just poked her nose into it and pushed through, but it was quite decidedly bumpy, and now and then a slant of rain would splash on to us. But that didn't matter a bit, we were quite warm and comfortable and were expecting very soon to be able to leave this little patch of nasty weather behind us.

At about II (Greenwich mean time) I glanced at the water circulation thermometer and saw that it was a good bit higher than it ought to have been, although we were still slightly climbing. It was clear enough that everything was not right with the water, as the temperature did not go down as I expected it to when I opened the shutters over the radiator a little. However, we carried on, but we didn't seem to be able to get rid of the clouds which now began to appear thicker and heavier than ever, and there was enough of them at lower levels to prevent any chance of our peeping at the sea.

By this time we had altered course a little to the northward, as from the information we had received at starting from the meteorological station we were expecting that the wind would tend to go more into that quarter. But it was none too easy for a decent course to be held, as the cloud formations we were running into were very formidable, and to say the least of it not without bumps. They were too high for us to climb over without;wasting a good deal of petrol which we wanted naturally enough to economise in every way, and another reason why we didn't want to climb was the increasing temperature of the water. So we just had to go round the clouds as best we could, but there were so many of them that Grieve never had a chance to take a sight on the stars.

A little later the moon rose and brightened things up and the outlook could do with a bit of brightening. The water temperature in the radiator had risen from 168 degrees to 176 degrees Fahrenheit, in spite of the shutters being quite wide open, and it was quite obvious that something serious was miss; otherwise the Rolls engine was running absolutely perfectly, the aeroplane was making no other complaints at all, and Grieve and I were happy and warm enough although the weather was so unkind.

At about 11.30 I determined that something had got to be done to keep the water temperature own, and had already reached the conclusion that the most probable cause was a collection of rust and odds and ends of solder and so forth that had taken loose in the radiator, and were stopping up the filter which prevents any solid substances from getting into the pump.

Very often one can get rid of this sort of stoppage stopping the engine and nose diving, so giving the accumulation a chance to spread itself and the filter to clear, with the rust and dirt at the bottom edge of it and not all over it. At any rate, there was nothing else to do, so down went her nose and we dropped quietly from 12,000 to about 9000 feet. I then started the engine up again, and was tremendously relieved to see that the temperature kept moderate although we were soon climbing again. But all the same our anxiety was not to be put aside, because if we had to do the clearing process often it meant that we should waste a lot of petrol, which with the wind a good deal against us we certainly could not afford to do.

An hour later, 12.30 p.m., the thermometer had returned to 175 degrees Fahrenheit. We were now about 800 miles out, and the weather had shown no signs whatever of improving, so that we were forced into continuing our cloud dodging tactics. Down went the nose again, but this time our luck did not hold, and when we started to climb up the temperature rose perilously close to boiling point. So we tried again, but things only got worse instead of better, and very soon the water started boiling in earnest.

We had nineteen gallons in the engine, but she was pulling about 200 horse power and once she started boiling, in spite of the intense cold—the atmosphere was getting on for zero—I knew it would not take long for the water to evaporate. After the second time of asking unsuccessfully I got the machine up to 12,000 feet and throttled her down, so that she would just about stop at that altitude so as give the water every chance.

The top plane was covered with ice from the radiator, and the steam was spouting out like a little geyser from a tiny hole in the middle of it. But for some little time we were able to keep the temperature just a little below the fateful 212 degrees.

There was now not much difficulty about keeping a course, for the moon was well up, and our 12,000 feet took us above most of the clouds, so that now and then Grieve was able to take an observaion on the stars which peeped out through gaps mostly to the northward. But about 6 o'clock m the morning we found ourselves confronted with a bank of black clouds as solid as a range of mountains and rearing themselves up in fantastic and menacing formations. They were at least 15,000 ft. high, so it was obviously useless to try and get over the whole lot, but when we couldn't fly round them—going through them was out of the question after we had had one try at it—we had a shot at going over some of the lower ones, but each time we rose the water temperature rose too, and furious boiling set in. So it was no good going on with that scheme.

In the meantime I had had no other trouble whatever in flying the machine. With the aid of the few stars we saw occasionally she was quite easy to trim, and when we got engulfed in the blackness of the clouds every now and then one was able to keep her level with the compass and the bubble.

Very reluctantly we came to the conclusion that as we couldn't go up we should have to come own, so we descended to about 6000 feet at about 6 a.m. Here it was blacker than ever, so down we went further and at about 1000 feet found things a good deal brighter with the cheerful sun just getting up to help us on our way.

Grieve's observations on the stars had shown that we were now on our course and well in the 'Steamer Lane.'

Water that constantly boiled even at 1000 feet did not help matters, and what showed us that we had really lost a great deal (if only we could have slung a bucket over board and picked up a few gallons as we went along!) was the fact that in our drop down we had had a very narrow squeak indeed. No sooner had the engine stopped than it must have gone stone cold owing to the small amount of water in the jackets, though steam was coming out of the radiator relief pipe quite merrily for some little time. This fact we had not realised until when quite low down I opened the throttle and got no response whatever.

I then shouted to Grieve to get busy on the petrol pump, and he was very soon bending forward and pumping hard enough to push the carburettor needle valves right off their seats and flooding the jets with petrol.

But nothing happened at all except that the Atlantic rose up to meet us at rather an alarming rate. We were gliding down wind at a pretty good speed, the sea was very rough, and when we hit it I knew very well that there was going to be a crash of sorts, and that if he remained where he was Grieve would probably get badly damaged, as he would be shot forward head first on to the petrol tank. So I clumped him hard on the back and yelled to him that I was going to 'land.'

We were then about 10 feet above the particularly uninviting looking waves.

And then we had the biggest stroke of luck.

Thanks to Grieve's pumping the engine at last fired, I gave her a good mouthful of throttle, she roared away with the best will in the world, the dive flattened and tilted into a climb and we were soon back again at a four-figure altitude and very glad to be there.

Had we hit the water we should have had not the slightest hope. Probably we would have been hurt owing to our speed with the wind, the aeroplane would have been badly damaged, and it as ten to one that if we had had sense enough left to launch the boat we shouldn't have been able to use it, and there was every probability of it being all over with us pretty quickly. I for one do not want a narrower shave.

Transhipping the aeroplane from the *Digby* to the *Portia* in Placentia Bay

By this time we had come to the conclusion that nothing could be gained by going on; we could still fly for an hour or two with what water we had left, but to get to Ireland was no longer within the range of practical politics, we had plenty of petrol, but the expenditure of water was what was critical. We now decided shortly after 6 a.m. to wander round in search of a ship. For this purpose we steered a sort of zig-zag course, dodging the clouds and squalls of rain, and keeping down low owing to the clouds. If we didn't spot one, then we had simply got to make the best landing we could, launch the boat, touch off our big Holmes flare which would last for an hour at least, and hope for the best. We also had plenty of Véry lights to fall back upon, and if it had got to be a long job we had plenty

Landing the aeroplane at St. John's

of food for we had scarcely touched any on the flight beyond drinking a fair amount of coffee and munching chocolate. Neither of us as a matter of fact had felt like eating at all.

We flew around for some two hours or so in weather that was getting a good deal worse rather than better. There was no lack of rain squalls, the wind was getting stronger and gustier and bumpier every minute, and the sea rougher. I was very glad to be without the under-carriage, and would rather have been as I was than have floats under me, for the waves looked too heavy for any ordinary seaplane to stand.

As may be imagined, I was not altogether without anxiety although I knew we were right on the steamer route, to which we had taken care to shape our course, because there was plenty of fog, and we might have passed quite close to a ship without seeing her.

Suddenly a hull loomed out of the fog and we knew that our luck, if it had been patchy, was at least good enough to stand up when the big strain came on it. I am ready to admit that I shouted with joy. Grieve says he felt like doing the same thing, but evidently the tradition of the Silent Service (to which he is an ornament) was too much for its vocal chords.

The hull belonged to the good ship *Mary* of Denmark, and she was sailing towards, for us, home. We flew around her and fired three Véry light distress signals and kept close by until her crew began .to appear on the decks. Then we hushed off a couple of miles or so along her course, judged the wind from the wave crests, came round into it and made a cushy landing in spite of the high sea that was running. The machine alighted jute nicely and, thanks to her partly empty tanks, rode clear of the water, although now and then the waves sloshed right over it and us and soon played havoc with the main planes.

However we had no difficulty in detaching our little boat and getting it launched, for the machine was sinking pretty fast, although we did not expect it would be likely to go down altogether.

Our life-saving suits worked splendidly and kept us quite dry. The *Mary* was soon close up to us and made speed to get a lifeboat out, but although, she was only two hundred yards off it was an hour and a half before she could get to us and take us off. They had run a line out to the boat from the ship and we were soon hauled in. Owing to the heavy sea it was impossible for us to salve anything, but as we now know a good part of the machine and the mail bag was afterwards picked up by the *Lake Charlotteville* and brought into Falmouth, so that our letters got delivered after all.

We were picked up on Monday at 8.30 p.m. Greenwich time (9.30 a.m. British summer time), fourteen and a half hours after we had started from Newfoundland.

Neither Grieve nor myself can possibly find words to express our deep gratitude to Captaino Duhn of the good ship *Mary*. His men had extreme difficulty in taking us off, and we owe our lives to their gallantry, for there is no doubt that, as Captain Duhn said, in another hour we should have gone down for keeps.

We had hoped to fall in with a ship equipped with wireless so that we could communicate with our people in England, and of this Captain Duhn, who spoke excellent English, thought we had a good chance, but later on the storm got considerably worse and he had to heave to, only making very little way in a northerly direction and so going further away from the busier shipping route:. So it was not until we were off the Butt of Lewis that we could communicate with home and the world that at one time had seemed so distant.

The Destroyer *Woolston* picked us up outside Loch Erriboll and took us to Scapa Flow, where we received a wonderful welcome from the Grand Fleet and Admiral Fremantle.

The next day we were put on terra firma and made the best of our way home. As to the reception we received and the demonstrations that were made, need I say that Grieve and I were more than deeply touched. We are completely agreed that the whole of this business was utterly undeserved and but of all proportion to what we had tried—and failed—to do.

The men who should have the reception are Raynham and Morgan, for what they did was a magnificent act of pluck. The east-north-east wind was not by any means a bad one for our getting off, for it suited our aerodrome pretty much as well as any other and better than most, but it was almost the worst possible wind for the Martinsyde aerodrome. But knowing this Raynharn and Morgan never hesitated to attempt the flight, and doing so they displayed a spirit and a courage for which Grieve and I have nothing but the most intense admiration and respect. They were visited with cruel hard luck indeed.

VI

NAVIGATION

BY H.G. HAWKER

Do not think it can be made sufficiently clear that in a flight such as that which we attempted, a non-stop journey of over 2000 miles, accurate navigation is of absolutely prime importance, and I am surprised, and I confess very disappointed to find that this point is so little understood that sufficient credit has not been given to the skill and the ability to overcome difficulties which was shown by my colleague, Lieut.-Commander Mackenzie Grieve. It is safe to say that given as I was a splendidly designed aeroplane, and a well tuned Rolls-Royce engine—the best aircraft engine in the world—there are thousands of pilots who are quite fit to perform the Atlantic flight, but as a writer in the *Times* put it, it is probable that the number of men in the flying services who are capable of doing the navigating of the transatlantic aeroplane could be counted on the fingers of one hand. Nothing could show this clearer than the fact that the American seaplanes got seriously off their course, although they were accompanied by a chain of destroyers acting as guide ships. Lieut.-Commander Mackenzie Grieve had nothing but difficulties to contend with, for no sooner had we left the hospitable shores of Newfoundland behind than we realised that so far as our wireless set was concerned it was going to be no use at all to us. This meant we had got to depend for keeping on our course entirely on observations of the stars, and to calculations on the dead reckoning principle. Apart from the fact that, as it happened in our case, observations of the stars were rendered practically impossible for hours on end by thick clouds, this form of navigation is exceedingly difficult in an aeroplane. The observer has very little room, and is bound to find himself cramped in using his sextant, so that unless he is extraordinary skilful in the way in which he handles is instruments he is likely to make serious errors.

On a short course this would not matter so much, but when you have to fly 2000 miles it must be borne in mind that an error of 5 degrees would put the machine 150 miles out at the end of the journey.

Then again height has to be allowed for. On board a ship this remains pretty constant, so that corrections are easily made, whereas in an aeroplane, as in our case, one's height can vary within an hour or two or less from 15,000 to 1000 feet. Height is taken from the barometer, but as the barometer reading alters according to atmospheric conditions, as well as being effected by height, a very big error can enter into this part of the calculation.

Then there is the question of cold to consider. For a good time during the course of our flight the temperature was zero or thereabouts. This did not worry me very much, as I was nicely tucked up underneath the cowling, but Grieve had to take his gloves off in order to use his instruments and make his calculations, and narrowly escaped getting serious frost bite in his fingers. I believe they were actually frost bitten, but in any case they must have been frightfully numbed, and it is a marvel to me that he was able to get through his intricate calculations in the way that he did.

Then, in connection with dead reckoning navigation he was confronted by other difficulties, the, clouds being, when we came to the worst part of our journey, so low as to make accurate drift observations very difficult indeed, and it is really wonderful that he was able in the face of these tremendous difficulties to keep us as close to our course as he did since when we struck the patch of really bad weather he was hardly able to make any observations at all. The NC 4 also suffered from navigational troubles in a manner and to an extent which only emphasises Grieve's wonderful work. On her flight to the Azores the NC 4 ran into fog, and for something like 170 miles, on account of the failure of her wireless, had to rely on dead reckoning. When her navigators were able to ascertain their position, they found that in flying this 170 miles they had got 45 miles off their course.

One thing, at any rate, is certain that for navigating a transatlantic aeroplane one wants a man whose skill and dependability is of the very highest, because the safety of the whole crew depends upon his work. I have no hesitation in stating that on a job of this kind, *the pilot owes everything to the navigator*, and I take this opportunity of publicly voicing my tremendous obligation and inexpressible admiration for Lieut.-Commander Mackenzie Grieve.

VII

THE NAVIGATION OF THE AEROPLANE

BY LIEUT.-COMMANDER K. MACKENZIE GRIEVE,
A.F.C., R.N.

The navigation of an aeroplane on long journeys over the sea presents a number of problems for which a sufficiently accurate solution cannot be found by any single method, but as in the case of a ship one means of navigation has to be used as a check on the other. I do not propose in these notes to deal exhaustively with the navigation aspect of aerial travel, because that would involve a rather long mathematical disquisition which I have no great desire to write, and I am sure very few people would have any desire to read. There are in existence plenty of books which deal very thoroughly with marine navigation, and practically the same conditions apply to aircraft as apply to ships. At the same time, since navigation is such an important feature of any long flight over the ocean, particularly the transatlantic flight, and as this is a science in which the average layman, and indeed the average pilot, has not hitherto taken much interest, it may be as well if I deal briefly with the more salient features of its practice. I am not suggesting, however, that it is a branch of knowledge which aviators must necessarily take up, for presumably most aeroplanes will be used in the future for comparatively short distance work, principally over-land routes, and in these circumstances the ascertaining of position is generally fairly easy, as landmarks, together with the reasonably accurate holding of a compass course, largely do away with he need for mathematical calculations. The lighter than air craft will, however, perform very long journeys over sea, for its future depends upon its capability of doing very long distances, and consequently an airship's navigation is as much a *sine qua non* as it is for every sea-going vessel which allows itself to get out of sight of land.

The first method of ascertaining one's position at sea, whether it be a ship or an aircraft that is in question, is dead reckoning. This involves a knowledge first of the direction of flight, and, secondly, of the speed of flight. If one is flying n perfectly still air and knows these two factors, the calculation of one's position is the acme of simplicity. All one would have to do in these circumstances would be to ascertain one's course by the compass, rule on the chart, or map, a line to represent it, and mark off upon it, according to he scale of the chart, the distance flown, which of course would simply be the air speed of the aero plane in miles per hour multiplied by the number's of hours one had been flying. For comparatively short journeys this fundamentally simple form of dead reckoning could be used, and in fact I understand it was used during the war for night bombing purposes in calm weather. But for long distances it would yield such inaccurate results as to be entirely out of the question.

Unfortunately, a great many variables enter into the matter, and prevent the navigator from arriving at the desired information in such an easy manner. The direction of flight as indicated by the compass is, in the first place, not necessarily the real direction, but, since it takes no cognisance of drift, only the relative direction; again, the speed of flight as shown on the air-speed indicator is not the real speed, or speed relative to the earth's surface, but only the speed relative to the air. Now the air is never still, and since the aeroplane is just as much affected by movements in the air as is a ship by currents in the sea, it follows that the direction of flight no less than the speed of flight can be affected very seriously by winds. If, for instance, the wind is constantly dead behind or dead ahead of the aeroplane it would have no effect upon the course, or rather direction of flight, and would simply affect the earth-speed of the machine. If, however, it is partly ahead, say, and partly from the side, it affects both the direction and the speed.

Hence it is absolutely necessary to introduce into the calculation a correction for the wind speed, which needless to say is constantly changing, as also its direction, and this can only be done by making observations of some more or less fixed object upon the earth's surface. Exactly the same state of affairs exists in the navigation of a ship by dead reckoning. The log gives the distance run and the compass gives the direction, but the result of a calculation from these two actors is not accurate enough for practical purposes until it has been corrected for currents, leeway, and errors in steering. In a ship this is a more simple matter than in an aeroplane, as the currents in the sea are relatively quite slow. Furthermore, they move generally in known directions and can consequently be represented on an ocean chart. Air currents are by no means so easily dealt with, because they are thoroughly irregular, both in speed and direction. It is true that there is a generally westerly trend of wind over the Atlantic, but this westerly trend is complicated by an infinite variety of local winds of every conceivable speed and direction which change, in respect of these qualities, at different heights above the surface. For instance, observations at meteorological stations upon winds at different altitudes frequently show that at, say, 500 feet there is an east wind of 20 miles an hour, and that simultaneously at 5000 feet there is a west or north wind of about the same speed. For the purpose of navigation over long journeys it is not sufficient to know the local speed and direction of the wind at the starting point, for by the time one has flown a hundred miles and climbed to 10,000 feet or so, the conditions will probably have changed altogether. A dead reckoning calculation made on the basis of the original wind condition. It being maintained would be utterly useless, as it might easily be subject to an error of 50 per cent in any direction.

Here I would desire to point out, for it is a fact that is not known to the extent that it should be, that once an aeroplane is in the air it is independent of all wind effects, that is to say, if the earth is out of sight the aviators have no means whatever of knowing either the speed or the direction of the wind. A great many people have an idea that if one is flying across a wind one is able to feel the wind on the side of one's face, exactly as if one were walking across a wind. This is not so: when they are flying the wind which the aviators can feel is always in the same direction, namely dead ahead, and is simply due to the speed of the machine. If they are flying with the wind they may be doing 150 miles an hour, if against it 30 miles an hour relative to the earth, but so far as the aeroplane is concerned its air speed remains the same no matter from what direction the wind comes. I hope I will be excused mentioning this elementary point: I only bring it forward because it relates to a fallacy which is extraordinarily widely held, and, indeed, is embraced by a number of people who ought to know better.

For the purpose of making an accurate dead reckoning we require to know the speed and direction of the wind. Incidentally I may remark that one of the principal reasons for maintaining a good altitude during a long flight is in order to take advantage of the fact that as greater and greater heights are attained atmospheric conditions tend to become more regular. If the surface of the earth, whether it be sea or land, is visible, an indication of the effect of the wind upon the course the

Difficulties of transport. The aeroplane stuck in the mud on the way to the aerodrome

aeroplane can be found by means of an instrument called a 'drift indicator.'

Supposing we had a circular hole in the floor of the aeroplane below the observer's seat, and across his hole there was stretched a string parallel to the fore and aft axis of the fuselage, then if there were no wind, or if the wind were dead ahead or dead astern, on looking through this hole we would see terrestrial objects rushing along in a direction exactly parallel to the string. But if there were a wind either entirely from one side, or partly so, one would see the earth moving at an angle to the string. If the string were now fixed in a new

Difficulties of transport. The aeroplane stuck in the mud on the way to the aerodrome

position, so that it lay parallel with the direction in which the ground was moving, the angle made between the new position of the string and the original axial one would be a measure of the drifting of the aeroplane, and from this angle one can arrive at the real direction relative to the earth in which the aircraft is travelling.

The drift indicator is an instrument which performs the same function as the string across the hole in the floor. It consists of a sighting arrangement, with or without lenses, crossed by parallel wires, and this is so mounted in the base of the instrument as to be easily rotated. It carries a pointer which reads off the angle of drift against a scale marked on the fixed base. Supposing, as shown in Fig 1 (overleaf), an aeroplane is flying due east and west from *A* to *B* at a speed of 100 miles per hour, and there is a northerly wind of 20 miles per hour, the difference between its real course and its apparent course will be represented in the diagram; the distance *AB* containing 100 units of distance, and the distance *BC* 20 units. Instead of keeping its due easterly course *AB* it will actually be flying in a southward direction along the line *AC* so that at the end of, say, an hour's run it will be at *C*, a distance of 20 miles from *B*, where it ought to be. The angle *BAC* is the angle of drift, and if one knows this from the drift indicator one can, knowing one's compass course, ascertain the direction of the line *AC*.

Having realised that in attempting to fly along the line *AB* he is actually flying along *AC*, the pilot can readily alter his course so as to bring him back to where he wants to be, or, on the other hand, if, as is generally the case, he gets a reading of his drift in the first half-hour or so of flight, he can keep to his desired course *AB* by making the necessary allowance for drift. If the angle *BAC* is 15 degrees, he will in this case steer 15 degrees north or due east along the direction *AF*, where his real course will become, with the drift influence, a due easterly one.

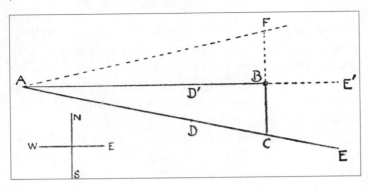

Fig. 1

But although the drift indicator gives one the direction of the true course *AC*, it does not, at the end of a run of so many hours, tell one exactly how far one has got along that line, since this course *AC* may be caused either by a wind coming, from due north or to a very much more powerful one coming either from north-east (that is to say partly *against* one), or from north-west (that is to say, partly *with* the aeroplane). In the former case one may, at the expiration of an hour, be at the point *D*, or in the latter case be at the point *E*, either of which is a long way from *B*. If one alters one's compass course to allow for drift as observed through the indicator, one will, therefore keeping on the course *AB*, be anywhere between *Dᵗ* and *Eᵗ*.

It is clear, therefore, that one requires to know more about the wind than a single reading of the drift indicator will tell one. By taking two readings on two different courses the speed and direction of the wind can be ascertained with reasonable accuracy. For this purpose two courses about 60 degrees apart, or more, can be adopted, one being, in the case of an east to west flight, 30 degrees to the north of the intended route; and the other 30 degrees to the south. For the first reading the aeroplane is steered, say, N. 60 degrees E., as shown by

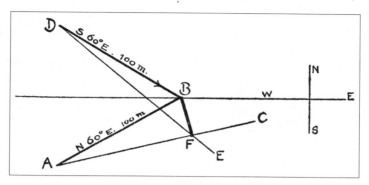

Fig. 2

the line *AB* in the diagram Fig. 2. The drift is now noted by observing the breaking crests of waves through the indicator, and the angle is found to be 10 degrees to the right of the compass course. This means that one's real course is along the line *AC*. The course is now changed and the aeroplane steered by compass to the direction of S. 60 degrees E., that is, in the erection of the line *DB*. In these circumstances he drift is found to be 5 degrees right, i.e. south, so that instead of going along the line *DB* one is actually travelling along the line *DE*. These lines are plotted on paper, making the length of the lines *DB* and *AB* proportional to the speed of the aeroplane, say 100 units in length, equivalent to a speed of 100 miles an hour. The line *DE* cuts the line *AC* at the point *F*. Then the line *BF* represents the direction in which the wind is blowing you, and the length of *BF* represents, in the proportion of its length to that of thy lines *DB* and *AB*, the force of the wind. For instance, If *BF* is one-fifth of the length of *AB*, the wind has a speed of 20 miles an hour, and its direction is from 'north and by west.'

The diagram makes it look as though an attempt to get the two flights along different courses demanded that the aeroplane should make both these flights in the direction of the point *B*.

This is because the angles have to be plotted in order to get the result. The actual course of the machine will be first along *AB* and then along a continuation of the line *DB*, starting from *B*. In the plotting this line is simply transferred to *DB*.

At night, drift can be taken from a flare dropped into the sea, providing the latter is visible.

VIII

ASTRONOMICAL OBSERVATION

LIEUT.–COMMANDER K. MACKENZIE GRIEVE

In the ordinary way one finds one's way about in a town by a process of dead reckoning, but in the event of the names of streets having been obliterated or a mistake having arisen in regard to the distance one has walked before having to turn to the left or to the right, one is forced into asking information from a policeman. Astronomical observation acts in much the same manner as such a policeman, as it serves check one's calculations. Furthermore, conditions may exist which make navigation by dead reckoning very difficult.

It is desirable from many points of view to fly at a considerable height. The weather conditions are apt to be far more stable at 10,000 feet than at 1000 feet, and this in itself is an important consideration. Then, on a long point to point non-stop flight, especially a flight over the Atlantic, it is necessary to economise fuel as much as possible, and this object is best served by keeping the aeroplane as high as she will reach on a fixed and limited throttle opening. Finally, there is the fact that if an engine or other failure demands a descent, a good altitude enables one to pick a landing anywhere within a considerable area. A gliding angle of 1 in 6, for instance, and an altitude of 10,000 feet give one a circle (the centre of this circle is altered in actual position according to the speed and direction of the wind) of roughly twenty-four miles in diameter to any point inside which one can get by a glide.

If, therefore, one maintains a good height it is obvious that clouds will interfere with one's observations of the earth's surface, and so possibly prevent one from obtaining any information as to drift. If one descends very low to get drift, observations one will have to expend a great deal of extra fuel in climbing up again, and apart from this one will still have to contend with the difficulty which I have already touched upon, namely, that the drift taken from a low altitude observation may not bear any definite relationship to the drift one is actually experiencing at a higher altitude.

As will be later explained, drift can be ascertained at night time, even when one is right above the clouds, by means of observations of the stars. But in daytime it can only be measured with the drift indicator.

But even if the sea is visible all the time it is highly desirable to have some means of checking one's computations, and for this purpose resort is had to astronomical observations. As navigation on this principle involves a great deal of mathematical calculations (the *modus operandi* of which is fully dealt with in standard text-books) it will be sufficient if I give a brief outline of the principle.

Positions are found by taking the altitude of the sun, or at night that of a star, above the horizon or level of the eye. The instrument used for this purpose is a sextant, and consists of a small telescope so mounted on a pivot as to be capable of movement in a vertical plane against a scale of angles. This arc must of course be held vertical. The principal difficulty to be dealt with is the fixing of a definite horizon, without which the angle cannot be measured. If one can see the sea horizon this is ideal, but one may not be able to do so owing to low-lying clouds. In these circumstances the horizon must be taken from the clouds themselves. Generally, such a horizon is dependable enough if the cloud sea is moderately flat and regular, but unfortunately this is not always the case by any means.

In our actual Atlantic attempt we met great difficulties in connexion with the cloud horizon except during the first four hours or so, when the cloud sea was almost perfectly flat and regular. Later on it developed a very irregular and Alp-like conformation, and under these conditions a very big error is naturally introduced into the calculations. At night time the cloud horizon has to be used almost exclusively owing to dimness of the sea horizon except when the weather is unusually clear.

When taking observations of heavenly bodies in a ship, one is always at a known height above the horizon from whatever point the sights are taken, and the correction for this source of error, which in any case is quite small for a ship, is made very easily. In the case of an aeroplane, however, it is not at all easy to state with accuracy exactly how high one is above the horizon one is using. If a sea horizon is being employed the aneroid, after being corrected for atmospheric temperature, gives one a sufficiently true reading of one's real height, but when a cloud horizon is adopted information on one's height above these clouds is not so easily got at, and a serious error can therefore creep in. Having got one's height above the horizon, the correction for it is made as follows: the square root of the height in feet is taken and the number so found represents minutes of angular measurement, and is subtracted from the observed altitude of the heavenly body that is being used. Suppose for the sake of example the last named, of the sun, is 45 degrees, and the height of the aeroplane is 8100 feet. The square root of 8100 is 90, so that 90 minutes, or 1 degree 30 minutes, has to be subtracted from the observed altitude, making 43 degrees 30 minutes.

Other corrections also have to be made for the reading given by the sextant. Thus there is a constant correction for the sextant itself, then there is a constant correction for the sun owing to the fact that the angle one requires is the angle of its centre, whereas the sextant observation is made either in the upper or lower edge of its disc, and finally there are corrections for refraction of the atmosphere and parallax. In the navigation of ships the last two factors have to be reckoned with, but in the case of an aeroplane they need hardly enter into the calculations to a serious extent, as even when the sun was very low they would only introduce a combined error of four miles or so in the calculated position.

Information as to the altitude of the sun, together with the exact Greenwich time (furnished by a chronometer) of observation, furnishes, if one knows one's latitude, the necessary data for the working out of a spherical triangle, the result of which gives an hour-angle of the sun, in other words the local solar time at the place of the observation. The difference between that time and the Greenwich mean time is a measure of the longitude, which is then converted into degrees, 15 degrees of longitude being equal to one hour of time.

If, therefore, one knows one's latitude one can by means of a single solar observation mark one's position on a chart with great accuracy. The fact that currents drive ships, and winds drive aeroplanes, off their courses, results in the fact that, in practice, one seldom knows one's latitude exactly.

One therefore has to assume a latitude. This together with the observed longitude gives one a point on the chart, and through this point one rules a line at right angles to the bearing of the sun at the time of observation, the angle of this bearing being given in tables.

This gives a 'line of position,' and one's actual place must be somewhere along that line. The line at right angles to the bearing of the sun could be obtained in another way by assuming two different latitudes, each of which, in conjunction with the sextant and time observation, gives a different longitude. These two points are then joined together, and give the required line.

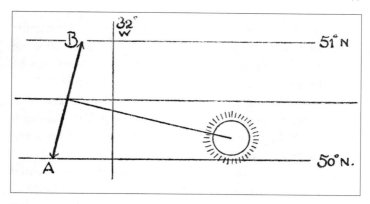

Fig. 3

This is made clear in the diagram Fig. 3. The bearing of the sun, on the assumption that one is in latitude 50 N., gives the position *A* in longitude; on the assumption that one is in latitude 51 N. it gives the position *B*. The line *AB* is the 'line of position,' and one's real position is somewhere along that line. The use of the tables enables one to rule the 'line of position' on the chart straight away on a single assumed latitude.

Having found our 'line of position' for one time, we run on for, say, a couple of hours and then take another observation of the sun, from which a second 'line of position' will be obtained, and this second 'line of position' will be at an angle to the first, owing to the fact that the sun has altered his bearing in the interval. We then fit in our run (allowing for drift) between these two lines, transfer the first 'line of position' to the end of the run, and our position is the point at which the second line cuts the first.

Referring to the diagram, Fig. 4 (p. 79):

At 6 a.m. the latitude is estimated (from the compass reading) to be, say, 50 degrees 30 minutes north, and then from this the longitude is found to be 32 degrees 30 minutes west. We know we are somewhere along the line *AB* which is at right angles to the sun's bearing. We then go on until 8 a.m., the length of run in this interval being, say, 200 miles, allowing for drift, and in the directions of east true. We should then be somewhere along the line *GD*, which is simply *AB* transferred to the end of the run. We now take a second sight, and from this we obtain the position line *EF*. Ruling this in, the point of intersection o the two lines gives our position at 8 a.m., say, longitude 29 degrees 30 minutes west.

At night navigation by astronomical observation is easier than by day, as instead of having a single heavenly body to work with there is an almost unlimited number. The position can be found by taking simultaneous or nearly simultaneous observations of any two stars whose bearing is sufficiently different to give a good and distinct cut at the intersection of the lines of position. By means of the stars both longitude and latitude can be definitely and directly established, whereas with the sun only this cannot be so easily done.

When the sun is on the 'Prime Vertical,' that is to say bearing east or west (true), the 'line of position' found runs due north and south, and is therefore the actual longitude, as it is itself a meridian. When the sun bears due south at noon, local time, the line of position gives the latitude, being itself a parallel of latitude.

In order to simplify calculations I used, in the Atlantic attempt, a diagram invented by Instructor-Commander Baker of Slough Observatory, as it away with the need of constantly working out triangles. Hence, with a few corrections, the line of position could be ruled direct on to the chart. The working being thus simplified, sights could be taken at short intervals and a continuous series of lines of position obtained, which, for the sun, would have the appearance shown in the diagram Fig. 5. The sun would bear, say, east at 6 a.m., south at noon, and, say, west at 6 p.m. The intermediate lines are at right angles to the bearing of the sun.

This is all very well for sea navigation, as the drift, due to current, bad steering, etc., is small, and the run between

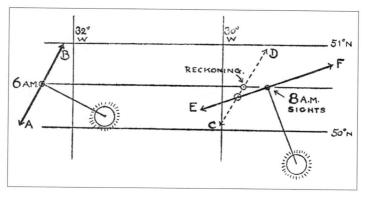

Fig. 4

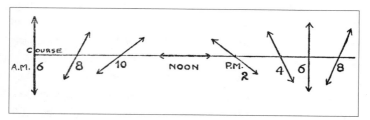

Fig. 5

observations can be calculated within very few miles by log and compass. In the air, the wind is highly variable, both in speed and direction, and may attain a velocity equal to more than half of the speed of the aeroplane. Thus beyond obtaining lines of position and knowing that we are somewhere on them, the information as to one's exact position is not complete, hence it is extremely difficult to obtain one's latitude except at about noon. For example, you reckon you have gone 200 miles due east between, say, 8 a.m. and 10 a.m. From this you get the result (1) shown in the diagram overleaf, Fig. 6. You may actually have gone 250 miles E.S.E., from which you would get result (2) as shown. One knows one is somewhere

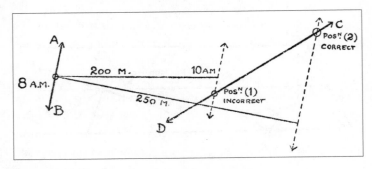

Fig 6

on *CD* at 10 a.m. by means of sights, but the intersection of this line of positon with *AB*, transferred to the end of the run, varies enormously with the estimate of distance, and with an incorrectly estimated run one may therefore be very many miles out.

Finding one's position in daytime, except longitude when the sun bears east or west, and latitude at noon, will always be difficult or impossible unless drift is known with reasonable accuracy. At night the stars can be used in order to provide the data for a calculation of drift.

As I have said, navigation at night time is much easier than by day, given a good cloud or sea horizon. In this connexion it may be mentioned that, proving he knows where to look for them, a navigator can, in daylight, get a sight on some of the planets, but for ordinary purposes planets have too much movement of their own to make them valuable for observation. At night the Pole star is invaluable. If he were situated above the true North Pole his altitude would give the latitude; actually he is not quite in this position, but apparently revolves round it. This involves a correction depending upon the sidereal time, which sometimes amounts to as much as about 70 miles, which has to be added or subtracted as the case may be. The height of the observer's eye above the horizon which is in use is required to be known. In order to ascertain drift it will not be necessary to come below the clouds as it would be in daytime, when there is only one heavenly body in sight.

For navigating purposes the moon is quite useless as far as aeroplanes are concerned, owing to its great speed through the heavens, and to the numerous corrections which have to be made for this body. As I have pointed out, navigation is simply a system of computation depending primarily upon speed and compass and, secondly, upon corrections by observation. A ship can get across the Atlantic quite easily by dead reckoning alone, helped by a chart of currents, and if a similar chart of winds were available to the aviator, no doubt an aeroplane could do the same. Unfortunately such a chart is almost unthinkable for altitudes of much less than about 50,000 feet, though above this height the winds tend to become quite regular and uniform, not only in direction but in speed also. Even more unfortunately, one cannot always get a sight at the stars or the sun. The conditions between air navigation and sea navigation are thus quite different. In the ship one can always use dead reckoning with quite sufficient accuracy, because one roughly knows the ocean currents, even when no heavenly body is visible for days on end. On an aeroplane one can fall back neither upon astronomical observation nor upon dead reckoning, since in the absence of any chart of wind currents the latter also requires observations, and such observations can be seriously interfered with by clouds.

As has been noted already, one cannot, at the present time, on an Atlantic flight afford sufficient petrol for a switchback course, now above the clouds, now below them, nor indeed is it a certainty that with the heavy load that such a flight involves one can actually get above them when one wants to. In our attempt we met with clouds of extraordinary density which extended from within about 2000 feet of the water to an altitude of at least 15,000 feet. These cloud masses were extremely irregular, and what made climbing, or even an attempt to climb, over them extremely difficult was the fact that they were produced by very violent local up-currents of air, as a natural result of which the clouds themselves were accompanied, on their flanks, by strong downward currents, through which the aeroplane could only mount at great expense of petrol. In these circumstances the observation of drift became extremely difficult, as for taking sights through the indicator one does not want to be down too low, and one was entirely prevented from taking the sights from the stars if we went through the clouds. We could only see the ocean occasionally through holes, or gaps, in the cloud sea below us. If an aeroplane is forced to fly through unbroken clouds for some little time, accurate navigation becomes practically impossible, owing to the fact that drift is an almost entirely unknown quantity. The only thing to do is note the courses that are being steered, and the time the machine is held on each, making such allowances for drift as one can.

IX

WIRELESS

BY LIEUT.–COMMANDER K. MACKENZIE GRIEVE

It is in such conditions as these that the potential value of directional wireless is seen. In ships it is not much used as yet, but just as in that connexion it will be useful in enabling a vessel to make land in a fog, so will it provide valuable information to an aircraft which is prevented from making observations either of the earth or of the heavens. If the transmitting wireless station is directly ahead or directly astern of one, it is sufficient to have, in addition to the compass; only a single station. Otherwise two, and preferably more, land stations are required. The position of the aeroplane is determined by the intersection of two lanes, the direction of each of which is dependent upon the position of the station sending the message. If the series of messages from one station is coming from a certain direction relative to the aeroplane, and a second series of messages from another station is coming from another direction, and these directions are known, the intersection of the two directions lines can be easily and instantly found on the chart, and that is the required position the actual apparatus the direction in which the waves are coming is ascertained by a telephone arrangement the noise of which reaches its maximum when the receiving part of they apparatus is pointing towards the source of message.

So far as our attempt was concerned the wireless apparatus was valueless, in fact we were not able to make any use at all of it, but that was not in itself a fault directly due to the design of the apparatus. As might be expected in equipping an aeroplane with wireless, many difficulties crop up which would not be met with at all on board ship, or in a land station. To start with, there is the need for economising weight in every possible way, there is none too much space to spare, and there is always a possibility—in our case it was more than that: it was an actuality—that the near presence of the magnetos of the engine will seriously interfere with the telephone apparatus upon which the directional part of the systems depends. We heard too many magneto noises to be able to distinguish the source of the messages sent from stations, but I understand that to a very large extent this difficulty has now been got over. Before leaving for Newfoundland we tried our aeroplane's speed, and the advantage of this directorial wireless apparatus at Brooklands, but was not successful and was therefore taken out of the aeroplane.

In the Sopwith machine the generator for transmitting messages is driven by a screw propeller, working in the relative wind due to the arrangement as that the generator need only be brought into action when required. When transmission of messages is not wanted the generator propeller can be drawn into the fuselage of the aeroplane, and it does not then consume any power from the engine. In some cases, especially in German aeroplanes, the generator is driven direct from the engine and a clutch is used for disconnecting it when desired. The former principle is preferable for this reason, that if the engine stops you have, in the latter case, no source of power at all, and consequently you cannot send out an S.O.S. whilst you are gliding down, whereas with a propeller-driven generator you can get full current developed by doing a sharpish dive.

As the generator screw is placed quite close—about 10 feet—behind the main screw, one would naturally suppose that when the aeroplane was climbing and the slip stream from the main screw was at its fastest the greatest current would be available, but as a matter of fact we found that this was not so at all, owing to the complicated system of eddy currents which evidently forms in the immediate neighbourhood of the fuselage. We several times tested the wireless generator drive with the aeroplane chocked up on the ground, when of course we ought to have got maximum power from it with the engine running fast, where as what really happened was that we did not get sufficient current for any practical purpose though when the machine was flying in the normal manner the drive should have worked all right. If you watched the generator propeller carefully you would see it suddenly almost stop and then buzz round again, so long as it was only being driven by the slip stream, but in they air it revolved quite regularly, showing that the thing that matters is the speed of the machine through the air rather than the speed of the slip stream.

The original wireless set in the Sopwith was a 'type 55 A' supplied by the Air Ministry. It had a range of about 200 miles. When we tried it in flight at Brooklands the Whittle belt drive was found to be slipping. The arrangement of the drive was then modified to take a silent chain in place of the belt. This was satisfactorily tested on the ground. It was not tried in the air until we got to Newfoundland, when trouble was early experienced owing to the exciter burning out (this appeared to be the most probable explanation) as a result of the screw driving the generator at too high a speed.

Mr Collins, the manager of the Marconi station at John's, to whom I am deeply indebted for many kindnesses which he showed us and the great deal of trouble he took on our behalf, furnished me with a 'Boy Scout' wireless set with a plain aerial. It had a range of about 25 miles, and for its type was quite satisfactory. It was installed in the machine in order to have something to fall back upon, but was afterwards taken out.

When the first wireless installation failed a cable was sent home for a completely new one, a 'type 52 A,' but unfortunately this did not arrive n time for it to be thoroughly tried in the air; in fact its first air test was carried out when we had left the shores of Newfoundland behind us, as it did not give a spark in the slip stream when the aeroplane was on the ground. When I tuned it upon that fateful Sunday evening I got a spark, but the amperage was very small, only .7 ampere. I have since been informed that this current ought to have been sufficient for a limited range, but I do not think we could have got an effective S.O.S. out at a speed much less than 80 knots. We were unable to make any wireless signal inasmuch as the trouble with the water circulation of engine did not allow the throttle to be opened to provide sufficient speed for the generator screw. The blade area of this we had slightly reduced, as we were afraid that the generator revolutions might be too high, and the exciter burn out as in the previous installation.

There is no doubt that for purposes of aerial navigation in the future, wireless telegraphy will be of the utmost value and importance, but I am of the opinion that for aeroplane work it will be difficult to attain the requisite degree of reliability unless some independent power plant is provide for driving the generator—a small separate petrol engine, for example, such as is used on airships If an air-screw is used it could be made much more reliable and effective if the blades were made adjustable, as with this arrangement it would be possible under any air conditions to keep the generator at an efficient but not excessive speed rotation.

It may be pointed out, for it is a matter that seems to have been generally misunderstood, that so far as receiving wireless messages to ships which can thus inform an aeroplane of its latitude and longitude, it is utterly useless unless the aviators can see the ship from which the signals are coming. If not, they may be under the likelihood of getting misleading information, for without knowing it they may be getting a position signal from a ship a couple of hundred miles away. This possibility

View of the Sopwith "Atlantic" machine, showing the air-screw for the wireless drive

can only be avoided by identifying the ship sending messages, by means of visible signals such as Véry lights.

Such being the case our wireless installation would have been of very little use to us, for owing to the weather conditions which were encountered, and to the fact that it was some considerable time before we got over the steamship routes, we never saw any ship at all until Hawker had the good fortune to spot the *Mary*. Even had it been working properly, our wireless set would have had its utility limited to the sending out of an S.O.S., which, under a merciful Providence, we did not have to fall back upon.

As I have observed, the second wireless set which we had was never tried in the air until we pushed off on our flight, and I do not entertain the least doubt that on the strength of this many people will say that we were taking an exaggerated and unjustifiable risk, and that we must have been absolute idiots to rely upon an untried installation. This is all very well, but if regard is had to the real conditions it will easily be seen that the thing is as broad as it is long, for the fact is that except under ideal conditions (which very rarely occurred) the aerodrome we had—or for that matter any aerodrome in Newfoundland—was so bad that to make any test flights at all was to take a serious risk with the aeroplane, and so far as the flight was concerned, we *were* counting upon the machine, and we were not counting upon the wireless, so that really we took the lesser of two evils.

X

SOME NOTES ON THE RUN

BY LIEUT.–COMMANDER K. MACKENZIE GRIEVE

So far as the actual navigation on our trip was concerned, all went well for a time and then serious difficulties came up in a formidable bunch. As soon as we had got well away from Newfoundland and had attained a reasonable height, I took observations of the drift through a hole in the clouds and found that this amounted to about 10 degrees. The course was therefore set on 80 degrees so as to bring us on to a real course of due east (true). The sun stayed with us up till about 10 p.m., Greenwich mean time, and whilst we had the sun we also had a good cloud horizon, the cloud sea being remarkably flat and regular, and so being quite ideal for observation purposes.

Unfortunately when the stars became visible the cloud horizon became so irregular as to make astronomical observations quite impracticable. There were great towers of clouds branching out of the main body, which was now almost completely without gaps, so that drift observations could not be taken.

At 10.15 p.m. we changed course, and steered another 15 degrees to the northward. The object of this was to bring ourselves over the steamer track. For this purpose our intended course yeas 73 degrees, less 8 degrees allowance for drift, so bringing the real course to 65 degrees. The reason I allowed less for drift was because the information we had received from the meteorological station in Newfoundland pointed to the probability of the wind getting, as we proceeded on our way, more and more into the north-west.

At 10 a.m. course was again changed to 55 degrees, as such scanty observations as I was able to get indicated that the drift had been considerably underestimated, and that we were 150 miles to the southward of where we ought to have been.

At 1.30 a.m. we changed course to 50 degrees, as the water circulation trouble appeared to be very obstinate, and our best chance for safety was to get on to the steamer lane with the least possible delay.

During most of the time we had been flying at about 10,000 feet with occasional descents.

From 1.30 a.m. till 5 a.m. the only observations it was possible to make were on the Pole star, as by good fortune there were occasional clear spaces in the clouds to the northward. We were this time dodging the higher cloud peaks, though the main horizon of the cloud sea was about on a level with our eyes. At 5 a.m. I was able to get sights on Arcturus and the Pole star, and ascertained our position to be latitude 49 degrees 30 minutes north, longitude 30 degrees west.

At 6 a.m. we gave up all hope of carrying on, as the engine had boiled most of the water away, and came down to look for a ship. This manoeuvre was very nearly attended with serious consequences our long glide clown from 10,000 to within a few unfired feet of the sea level the engine, owing to the fact that there was very little water in the tickets, became stone cold and refused to start when It was switched on. I accordingly got busy with the petrol force pump in order to flood the carburettors, and had been working hard at it for a few moments when Hawker tapped me on the head and shouted to me to sit up as we were going to land, and in my crouching position I might get badly knocked about if we hit the water hard. This we were very likely to do, as it happened at is time that we were gliding with the wind. Heaven be praised, the gallant Rolls-Royce engine rose to the occasion and responded just in time. We were within about twenty feet of the ocean when, the first gloriously welcome splutter came down the exhaust pipe, and not much above ten feet altitude by the time the twelve cylinders had taken up their duties.

After that little incident, which would certainly have been the end of us if the engine had finally refused, we rose to 2000 feet and set about looking for a ship, dodging the low clouds, and running into squalls of rain. The weather at this time was rapidly getting worse and the sea more rough.

We were very glad indeed to see the *Mary*!

It is more than probable that the great error—150 miles—in our reckoning was not entirely due to the fact that the bad weather conditions after 10 p.m. made observations difficult, as it is quite likely that the error was to a certain extent present in my calculations from the very start.

As will have been gathered from what I have said already, navigation of an aircraft involves a certain amount of work which must be carried out with great care and accuracy, otherwise big errors will creep in and completely stultify results. On an aeroplane the work is not rendered any easier by the fact that one's quarters, to say the least of it, are pretty cramped. So far as warmth was concerned I had nothing to complain of, for our suits kept us quite comfortable, until I had to make an observation with the sextant, and then conditions were not quite so good, as the working of this instrument and the subsequent calculation meant taking one's gloves off. My silk gloves which I wore next the skin managed to get themelves blown overboard. From about 10 p.m. to 5 a.m. we were frequently at an altitude of 10,000 feet or more, and the temperature was somewhere about zero Fahrenheit. Whilst messing about with my instruments I suppose I was lucky not to get badly frost-bitten,—as a matter of fact I did get a touch which numbed my fingers for a week or two. What was even more distressing was the fact that my handkerchief got frozen as stiff as a board!

The small space in which one can move does not make the taking of sights any easier than it might be, for to use one's sextant involves, like some of the machine guns fitted on the early aeroplanes in the war, a good deal of neck twisting and looking round the corner. A buffeting eddying slip stream does not conduce to holding the instrument steady, and one has to brace oneself as stiffly as ever one can. The main point is to have instruments upon which one can place absolute dependence. In this respect our machine was well served, at all events, everything was of the very best procurable quality; but even so trifling faults made their appearance, though none of them, with the exception of the wireless installation trouble to which I have referred, amounted to very much. The compass developed a bubble, as compasses not infrequently do.

I had intended to use an aerial sextant of a special pattern which had been invented by Instructor-Commander Baker of Slough Observatory. Bt this unfortunately must have been dropped in transit, as when it was unpacked a lens was found to be broken, and even after a repair had been effected the error of the instrument due to this mishap was too large to allow of its being used. This sextant had the important advantage of doing away with the need for estimating the height of the observer's eye above the horizon. I actually used an ordinary sextant which I bought in Newfoundland.

I kept a diary of my observations, but unfortunately this, with the exception of a single leaf, was washed out of the aeroplane. It contained no particularly valuable information, but it would have been an interesting souvenir. In it I made notes of heights and air speeds taken every half-hour, and details of observations on drift, sun and stars, etc.

It is only natural that the question should arise, has anything been learned from this transatlantic attempt? I am scarcely qualified to speak about any technical aspects other than those relating to navigation, but my view is that so far as this department is concerned there are at least a few things that have been pretty definitely established.

It has been shown that, within limitations, the Atlantic can be successfully navigated by observations of the celestial bodies using a cloud horizon. It must, in this connexion, be borne in mind that the same degree of exactness is not demanded in the navigation of an aircraft as in the case of a ship. Fog and haze render the visibility near the surface of the sea very bad, and in addition to that it is necessary for a ship to use much greater care in making land than the aeroplane need. There are rocks in the atmosphere and the choice of landing grounds, or what can be used as landing grounds when the occasion arises, is much wider than the choice of harbours.

It has also been shown—a fact to which I think importance can be attached—that great continents of clouds can be met which prevent other means of navigation being employed and render wireless assistance absolutely necessary.

It will certainly be interesting to compare our experience with that of others who, I hope, will be more successful than we were.

In conclusion, I would desire to place on record an appreciation of the qualities of my very good friend, H.G. Hawker. To my mind he is an ideal pilot, with unlimited pluck, unfailingly good judgment, and what is equally to the point, an inexhaustible supply of good spirits. In his handling of an aeroplane I am tempted to believe that he takes advantage of some sixth sense which allows him to become an integral part of the machine but I do not know whether to admire him more in this capacity than in his ability to support, with a characteristically cheerful philosophy, the almost intolerable tedium of waiting in Newfoundland for something which meant even more to him than to me.

XI

THE SINGLE-ENGINE AEROPLANE

BY H.G. HAWKER

In some quarters considerable wonder has been expressed that we attempted the long flight across the Atlantic with a single engine aeroplane, and it has even been said that because we had only the one motor to rely on we were taking unnecessary risks which might have been reduced had the design of the machine incorporated two or three, or even more power-plants. It seems to me that there is more misconception about this multiple-engine proposition, and more nonsense talked about it, than anything else connected with aeroplane design.

The opinion seems to be quite widely held that if you have four or five engines to carry on with, you are morally bound to get safely to your destination, even though one or two of these engines should break down *en route*. As a matter of fact this is very nearly a complete fallacy, and I myself am quite satisfied that so far as reliability is concerned, a single-engine aeroplane is a match for any multiple-engine machine.

In the first place, I believe that there is not a single multiple-engine aeroplane which with full load of petrol or passengers can fly with anything less than all its engines in operation. Now in a job like the crossing of the Atlantic your aeroplane has got to carry the greatest possible load because you want every pint of petrol that you can get aboard, to say nothing of wireless apparatus, and other odds and ends, all of which in the aggregate make a considerable weight. Therefore if a three- or four-engine aeroplane has got to use all its motors to fly, it is not in the least any better off than a single-engine aeroplane. Both machines are equally dependent on all their motors keeping going. Of course if you are going to have a huge machine to carry a trifling load, say enough petrol for two or three hours only, it is quite feasible to fly with two motors out of four running, but loads of this sort are no use whatever for an Atlantic flight, and I am strongly of the opinion that they would not be much good for commercial purposes either. I need hardly say that commercial aeroplanes are scarcely likely to be called upon make non-stop flights of a couple of thousand miles. That sort of journey can probably be better done with an airship.

As a matter of fact, I do not think there is very much question that, having regard to the conditions under which they work, the engines of a multiple power-plant aeroplane are likely to be less reliable than that of a single-engine machine. The reason or this is that the former is less efficient than the latter owing to the head resistance of the engine eggs, and the additional weight of structure which is involved by fixing the motors on the wings instead of in the fuselage. Such being the case, at ordinary cruising speeds, the multiple engines will have to run at a bigger throttle opening than is the equivalent case with a single-engine design, other things being equal. I need hardly say that the life, and consequently the reliability, of any engine is impaired very considerably if it is constantly run at a big throttle opening. If you want to cover a very big distance non-stop, your machine must be designed so that it will fly quite comfortably with the engine never going more than half its full power. On a multiple-engine aeroplane carrying full load this cannot easily be done.

I am the first to admit that the American aeroplane NC 4 did a magnificent performance in achieving the distinction

Mr Raynham and his Martinsyde starting for a trial flight

of being the first aeroplane to make the complete journey between America and Great Britain, but this feat does not argue that the four-engine machine is any better than the single-engine type, for it will be remembered that originally four multiple-engine aeroplanes were constructed especially for the American effort. Of these one met with an accident at Rockaway. Of the three which started from Newfoundland, only one, the NC 4, got to the Azores without mishap, showing very clearly; that this big type of machine is just as dependent upon all its engines running without trouble as the smaller single-engine aeroplane.

There is another reason too, which accounts for the fact that Mr T.O.M. Sopwith and all off those associated with him are convinced of the commercial future of the single-engine aeroplane. If aerial transport is to be successful it must be economical. This means, firstly, that the machine has got to be efficient, which from its very construction a multiple-engine machine cannot be to the same extent as the single-motor type; and, in the second place, it has got to carry as big a proportion as possible of its total weight in the air in the form of 'useful load,' i.e. petrol, passengers, mails, cargo, etc. As the size of aeroplanes is increased, their structural weight is also increased, and makes inroads upon the weight that can be disposed of in cargo. In our Sopwith 'Atlantic' machine the useful weight was more than half of the total weight, a very much higher proportion than any multiple-engine aeroplane can show for an equal distance capacity.

Still another reason why, for purposes such as the Atlantic flight or any other non-stop flight of a similar distance, a machine of the highest possible efficiency must be employed is that fuel must be used as sparingly as possible. If the wireless apparatus goes wrong, as it did in our case (and also in the case of one of the American flying boats), the only way of navigating the machine with any accuracy demands that an altitude be reached which is well above the highest clouds, otherwise observations cannot be made of the stars. Under conditions of bad weather a machine of low efficiency might be forced into the necessity of relying entirely on its wireless, and it is clear that this apparatus, so far as aeroplanes are concerned, has not reached as yet the high standard of dependability which is demanded if it is to be the sole means of navigation, though it will no doubt reach this one day in the near future. The NC 2 and NC 3 aeroplanes both lost themselves between Trepassey and the Azores because their wireless gear went wrong, and they were unable to climb out of the fog and above the clouds so as to make astronomical observations.

Let it not be supposed that my advocacy of the single-engined aeroplane implies that I am not in favour of making more powerful aeroplanes. Far from it. I am quite certain that in the near future the power of aeroplanes will be much increased, but the point is that this does not necessarily mean a multiplication of separate power plants. We shall want single engines of 1000 h.p possibly of 2000 h.p., and when we have got them I do not doubt that we shall be able to turn out moderate-sized aeroplanes that will show a good economy whilst still retaining high speed, a good speed range (so that they will not want aerodrome of huge size), and what is of great importance, a big capacity for load carrying. I am aware that there are difficulties in the way of making very high-powered engines of light weight, but what are these difficulties compared to those which uses to crop up in the early days of aviation and which have been completely overcome and are now entirely things of the past?

For commercial work involving pretty long distance trips over sea or over country in which landing is difficult, or where the weather is inclined to be fractious and unreliable, I have great faith in the powerful single-engined machine, because it gives one a much bigger range of altitude, so enabling one to take better advantage of favourable winds, or to cheat unfavourable ones, rendering navigation much easier, because the ability to get to a big altitude means that one can get over any cloud that will be ordinarily met with, and providing altogether better conditions for flying.

Perhaps Grieve might not agree with 'altogether better conditions for flying,' for 10,000 feet at night time is too cold for comfortably working a sextant, and 20,000 feet will be keener still. But I dare say his experience, and the experience of other navigators, will lead to the invention of instruments which can be operated with fingers muffled up in warm gloves so that frost-bite is no longer to be feared.

There is one point that I think might be touched upon in a consideration of aeroplanes with multiple engines; it is this, that from the point of view of the public, which, very naturally, is not brought into touch with the technical side of aeronautics, there is a strong likelihood of the airship being regarded as just a similar sort of thing to an aeroplane. No one in their senses could possibly deny that on lighter than air craft multiple engines are desirable in every way, and I dare say that in the minds of a good many this is a good argument for their use on aeroplanes. But really the cases are quite different. In an airship the whole of the engine power is utilised in propelling the aircraft forward, and none of the engine power is required for sustaining the machine in the air. In an aeroplane only a fraction of the power is used for actual propulsion, most of it being consumed in overcoming the resistance which is converted into a lifting effect on the wings. Consequently in an airship the only thing that happens when one, or more, engines go out of action is that the speed as to be reduced. The airship still goes on flying all right, and very likely the engine trouble can be put right there and then. But the failure of one engine on a multiple-engine aeroplane may easily mean that the machine has got to come down perhaps not suddenly, but probably slowly.

But even if it is just able to fly with less than the full complement of engines, it is quite certain that those which are in action will have to be run at pretty full throttle to overcome the resistance of the idle screw, and if that is done there is all the more chance of one of the survivors breaking down.

XII

DROPPING THE UNDER-CARRIAGE

BY H. G. HAWKER

Whilst we were in Newfoundland we were quite amused to read some of the newspaper comments upon our chance of doing the big flight, and from this it was quite evident that very few newspaper men know what they are talking about when they have to deal with flying matters. In several quarters it was suggested that the idea of Mr Sopwith letting us use an aeroplane from which the under-carriage was to be discarded in mid-air was, to say the least of it, very scandalous, and it was confidently said that even if we got right across the Atlantic we should probably smash ourselves to pieces in making a landing on the bottom of the fuselage.

As a matter of fact, it was I myself who persuaded Mr Sopwith to adopt the detachable under-carriage idea. The Atlantic is a very big thing, and we wanted all the margin of distance that we could possibly have for our machine, that is to say, we wanted to save all the petrol we could, and we also wanted to get all possible speed without making our petrol consumption excessive. In other words, what we had to do was to save weight and head resistance, and both of these objects could be secured by getting rid of the under-carriage. Except at the beginning and the end of the flight, the landing gear is just so much useless weight, and useless resistance. With the wheels and axle of the machine our speed with the petrol consumption of 15 gallons per hour was 105 miles, but without the under-carriage the speed at the same petrol consumption was 112 miles per hour, an increase by no means to be despised.

If I were to say that I considered the machine would actually be safer without an under-carriage than with one I dare say I would be accused of a slight exaggeration, but it would be true enough if I had even considered the possibilities of failure. Of course one always has to consider possibilities of failure to a certain extent, it would be madness not to do so, but I know that my belief that we should do the trip all right was very well founded. So it was a case of the probabilities of success and the possibilities of failure, and in this connexion I would only say that my faith in the Sopwith machine and the Rolls-Royce engine—the best aeroplane and the best motor—has by no means been shattered, and the only pity is that the Atlantic is such a big thing that one can't very well have another go at it when the first attempt has not come off. But what I want to convey is that in the event of failure, which would mean landing on the water, we were very much better off without an under-carriage than with one. Ordinary land aeroplanes that alight on water invariably turn head over heels, because the wheels stike the water first, and the tremendous resistance that they meet with forms such a big force that no amount of pulling back the stick can possibly prevent the machine from putting its head into it with such a crash that very likely the pilot and navigator will be killed outright or, what amounts to pretty much the same thing, knocked unconscious perhaps for hours.

I reckoned that if anything brought us down some distance away from a ship it would be very necessary for us both to have all our wits about us. We could not be quite certain how the machine would float, and the cockpit might get submerged very quickly or it might not, but in any case what was certain

The Sopwith wreckage on board the SS *Lake Charlotteville*

was that we should have to launch our little boat and get busy with flares. So it was eminently necessary to drop on the water as softly as possible.

As to making a landing on the ground, whether it was to be the coast of Ireland or Brooklands, there was no need to worry at all. The old Wright pilots always used to prefer to land on their skids rather than on wheels, and the bottom part of our fuselage was much the same shape as the old Wright skids.

There is no difficulty about getting off with an under-carriage, and dropping it from the machine when one is well clear of the ground. In our machine, the axle and under-carriage struts were comfortably held into sockets by means of a single tension-wire fitted with a release device connected up to a small lever, so that when we had got fairly started, all I had to do was to pull this trigger, and the under-carriage immediately said 'Good-bye' to the aeroplane. As the weight of the axle and wheels was very nearly under the centre of gravity of the aeroplane, the loss of the under-carriage made practically no difference to the balance of the machine, and, in fact, when I had actually dropped the axle I simply did not feel it go, though when we looked over the side Grieve and I could see it spinning down towards the sea.

Once you have got rid of your under-carriage the only difficulty that presents itself is that of landing. Contrary to popular belief this is by no means a serious difficulty. On a good ground one should not have to do much damage to the wings, though if one has a four-bladed propeller, one has got to reckon with smashing at least two of the blades off. If when one cuts one's engine off a two-bladed propeller remained horizontal, it need not get broken, but the question of smashing the propeller is trifling in comparison with the advantage of dropping the under-carriage.

On a rough aerodrome the landing would be a bit bumpy, no doubt, though it would not be any more dangerous than an ordinary landing, as it is almost impossible to imagine that the aeroplane could turn over. The shape of the bottom side of the fuselage is quite ideal for running over the ground, and on our machine the fuselage longerons were reinforced with strong wooden runners. I have not the slightest doubt that if better fortune had allowed me to get to Brooklands, or even to Ireland, I could have landed the aeroplane without doing much damage either to it or to ourselves.

But the thing which, above everything else I think, determined the use of a detachable landing gear was the difficulty of the aerodrome in Newfoundland. We knew very well from the nature of the country that the best aerodrome we could possibly find, leave alone the fact that when Captain

Montague Fenn went out to discover one the whole place was under snow, would be a very bad one, and that to allow for this the under-carriage had got to be far stronger, and therefore far heavier than would be wanted for Brooklands or Hendon, or even an ordinary patch of Irish pasture land. The heavier we made the wheels and axle, the worse would be their effect upon our speed and petrol consumption in the air, so if we were prepared to gain a little on the swings, i.e. the safety of getting off, not only for the big attempt, but also for trial flights, we should have to yield a big lot on the roundabouts, and this last loss would be felt every minute of the twenty-four or so hours' flight. In my opinion, and, in spite of the water circulation trouble which we had, it is my opinion now as it was then, that the worst trouble we had to contend with was the aerodrome. But I have dealt with that more fully in another chapter.

XIII

HELP FROM SHIPS

BY H.G. HAWKER

It appears that when we had fallen into the Atlantic and no news had been received of us in Great Britain, a considerable outcry was raised in certain quarters against the fact that on our flight we were entirely unaccompanied by ships, and bitter comparisons were made between the organisations for the transatlantic flight made respectively by the British and by the American Navies. As there still seems to be a good deal of misunderstanding on this point, it may be just as well if I make the whole matter as clear as possible.

In the first place, there is absolutely no similarity between the transatlantic flight of the American seaplanes and the attempt of Lieut.-Commander Grieve and myself on our Sopwith. The first was a national affair. The Americans, or rather the aeronautical authorities in the U.S.A., had made up their minds that to be the first country to send an aeroplane from America to Europe was an honour well worth a big national effort. Consequently they organised the whole thing on a magnificent scale, reduced the likelihood of failure to a minimum, sent out a big escort of ships, got four machines ready for the flight, and generally did not scruple to spend a great deal of money. It cannot be too strongly insisted upon that this did not in the least detract from the honour of what the NC 4 achieved. It simply means this, that the Americans thought so much of the transatlantic flight that they went in for it on a national basis, whilst the British authorities did not see eye to eye with them in this matter. The consequence was that so far as British aviation was concerned its prestige was left in the hands of private enterprises, such as the Sopwith Aviation Company, Messrs Martinsyde Ltd., Handley-Page Ltd., Vickers Ltd., etc. All of these firms had entered for the *Daily Mail* £10,000 prize whereas the Americans were not entered for the prize, and consequently could organise their flight on entirely different lines.

The idea of the seaplanes being accompanied by ships was a perfectly good one, inasmuch as the NC machines could 'land' anywhere they liked between the shores of America and Europe, and it must be clearly remembered that their flight was also undertaken with a view to research work. The U.S.A. Navy was anxious to get all possible information upon aerial navigation on long flights, and they were well justified therefore in taking every possible precaution to secure the safety of the personnel on their machines. For our part, ships, except those of the ordinary mercantile marine, from which we hoped to get wireless reports, did not enter into the programme at all. Our Sopwith was a land machine which, if it were brought down to the water, could not rise from it; consequently a chain of ships would have been very little use to us if they had been sent out. But we did not want them sent out. As I have said, ours was a private enterprise, and it would have been a little too much to expect the long-suffering British taxpayer to foot the bill for keeping fifty or sixty warships in a chain across the Atlantic for many weeks on end. We had to wait in Newfoundland for nearly two months before we could make a start, and the vessels would therefore have had to be at sea all this time. They certainly could not have remained in harbour until they heard from us that we were ready to start, because the fastest of them would take a day and a half to get from Ireland to anything like

The wreckage brought ashore at Falmouth

mid-Atlantic, and by that time if all had been well the flight would have been over, or the weather might have changed and the flight have had to be postponed.

When I had the honour of being received by His Majesty the King at Buckingham Palace, it was a great pleasure for Grieve and myself to be able to assure him that this public outcry for Admiralty help was all nonsense so far as we were concerned, and that we had never wanted any such help, and had not in the least relied upon receiving it.

Personally, I am one of those hardened believers in the future of aviation who hold that this latest means of transport

Side view of the Sopwith "Atlantic" Aeroplane

will demonstrate its ability to remain absolutely independent of any other form of transport whatever. It ought to be possible to navigate an aeroplane from one point to another without any help from ships, I and have no doubt that in the not far-distant future, when directional wireless has been more highly developed, this will actually be the case.

I need hardly say that when we were forced to realise that a complete flight was impossible, we were very glad to take advantage of the safety afforded by the first ship we found, but that was only because our attempt failed. Who could doubt that some day in the future the failure of aeroplanes to get to their destination will be so rare that complete success will be absolutely the rule?

I have thought all along that so far as the Atlantic flight was concerned, the problem was to get from St. John's, Newfoundland, to some point in Great Britain with a total disregard of what lay in between. It might be land, it might be water, it might be boiling oil: if the aeroplane is what we want it to be it does not matter what sort of stuff is to be flown over. Then, again, one must bear in mind that our Sopwith was a very different machine from the NC seaplanes. As a matter of fact the latter had only two methods of navigation open to them, whereas we had three. They are heavy machines, and as aeroplanes not very highly efficient, consequently they could not rise to a very great height so as to be able to get above high clouds for the purpose of making astronomical observations. They therefore had to navigate either by directional wireless or by dead reckoning, or both. The NC 4 had a good deal of trouble on the way, but it did the journey all right, although it took some time about it. That, however, is not the point. The NC 4 has attained a place in aeronautical history because it is the first seaplane to fly across the Atlantic, and realising as I do the tremendous difficulties of this great flight, it gave me particular pleasure to form one of those who met Commander

Read at Plymouth to congratulate him on his feat and to welcome him and his crew to this country. I would, however, like to point out that a great deal of the credit for the American success belongs to Commander Towers, who was responsible for the whole of a magnificent piece of organisation. When the four NC machines were in Newfoundland we tried to get over to see them, but Trepassey was too far off, and the means of communication between there and St. John's were such that we could not have got there and back in reasonable time, and we were anxiously waiting almost every minute for the weather to show itself sufficiently good for a flight.

When in January Mr Sopwith, Mr Smith, the designer of the Atlantic machine, Mr Cary, and myself and others were discussing the entry for the great competition, we had to consider whether we should design a seaplane for the job or use a land machine. After much careful thought the opinion was unanimously come to that a land machine should be used, and the whole flight attempted in one big hop. We believed then and we implicitly believe now the ability of a good machine to do the journey non-stop under reasonably favourable conditions, and we were only too ready to show to the public our complete faith in the reliability of aeroplanes and aeroplane engines. The fact that Grieve and I were brought down in the Atlantic by water circulation trouble does not in the least affect this confidence. Trifling mishaps like this are really out of all proportion to their consequences, and if I were to make another attempt, and in this I know that Commander Grieve entirely agrees, then we would go on a single-seater land machine as we did before.

XIV

NOTES ON THE AEROPLANE

BY H.G. HAWKER

The Sopwith 'Atlantic' aeroplane which, with its Eagle VIII Rolls-Royce engine, carried us so splendidly in the attempt on the big crossing was designed and built by the Sopwith Company in six weeks, as the firm had been so busy with Government work that they were not able to devote attention to designs intended for civil flying. It was constructed, especially in regard to the boat forming the tipper part of the fuselage, the detachable under-carriage, and the tanks, primarily for the Atlantic attempt; but very slightly modified and under the name of the 'Sopwith Transport' it has all along been intended to become a definite commercial model. Its general lines will easily be gathered from the photographs, and the following are some of its principal dimensions and performance figures:

Span	46 ft. 6 ins.
Length over all	31 ft. 6 ins.
Chord	6 ft. 3 ins.
Gap	6 ft. 0 ins.
Total surface	550 sq. ft.
Loading per square foot	11.2 lbs.
Load per horse power at 360 h.p.	17.1.
Cruising speed, using 15 galls. per hour	105 m.p.h.
Speed	118 m.p.h.

"The finest engine in the world." The 360 H.P. Eagle VIII Rolls-Royce
Aircraft Engine

Speed at 10,000 ft. altitude	105 m.p.h.
Maximum endurance	31 hrs.
Total weight	6150 Ibs.
Useful weight (other than engines and structure tans, etc.)	3350 lbs.
Ratio of useful weight to total weight	54.4 per cent.
Ceiling	13,000 ft. (when fully loaded).
Horse power	360 h.p.

XV

NOTES ON THE ENGINE

BY H. G. HAWKER

The following particulars relate to the Eagle VIII Rolls-Royce engine, which I never hesitated to describe as the 'finest engine in the world.' I never entertained any doubt about the ability of an aeroplane to do a single flight right across the Atlantic, providing the engine were a Rolls-Royce.

Type

12 cylinder, vee, water-cooled.

Bore	4 ½ inches.
Stroke	6 ½ inches.

Power, Speed, and Fuel Consumption

Normal brake horse power	360 h.p.
Normal crankshaft speed	1800 r.p.m.
Normal propeller speed	1080 r.p.m.
Fuel consumption	24 gallons per hour.
	55 pints per h.p. hour.

Weight

Engine complete, excluding reduction gear, exhaust boxes, radiator, oil, fuel, water and starter battery	836 lbs.
Engine as above, including reduction gear	900 lbs.
Weight per horse power	2 ½ lbs.

We used Wakefield's Castrol 'R' lubricating oil, K.L.G. sparking plugs, 'F. 12' and Shell petrol. Each and all are the very best of their kind, and none of them failed in the smallest degree.

ALSO AVAILABLE FROM NONSUCH PUBLISHING

—•—

For forthcoming titles and sales information see
www.nonsuch-publishing.com